Using Digital Portfolios to Develop Students' Writing

This book equips pre-service teachers, research postgraduate students, teacher educators, and language specialists with specific knowledge and skills about the principles, research, and applications of digital portfolios within the EFL writing contexts.

While most digital portfolio scholarship focuses on higher education, this book targets primary-level and secondary-level school audiences, namely pre-service teachers, teacher educators, and Ministry of Education staff members with a focus on EFL writing. The rationale behind this design is that the published literature on digital portfolios tends to be generic and one-size-fits-all; there has been scant published scholarship about the development of digital portfolio literacy among teachers and pupils, which could enable them to upgrade the teaching and learning of writing in a larger EFL environment. This volume fills this gap by illustrating the why, what, and how aspects of digital portfolios in ten reader-friendly chapters.

Guiding educators to enrich their pedagogical repertoire via the portfolio approach, this book emphasises a healthy balance between principles, research, and practice. It is an easy-to-follow guide to setting up digital portfolio systems and coaching pupils to improve writing, ensuring the dissemination of digital portfolios with high fidelity.

Ricky Lam is Associate Professor and Associate Head in the Department of Education Studies at Hong Kong Baptist University, Hong Kong, China. He is Associate Editor of *Frontiers in Psychology* and has served in several international editorial boards of journals, such as *Assessing Writing*, *RELC Journal*, and *Journal of Asia TEFL*. He has mentored eight doctoral students.

Benjamin Luke Moorhouse FHEA is Assistant Professor in the Department of Education Studies at Hong Kong Baptist University, Hong Kong, China. He is a recipient of the Early Career Teaching Award 2019 from the University of Hong Kong and a Fellow of Advance HE.

Routledge Research in Language Education

The *Routledge Research in Language Education* series provides a platform for established and emerging scholars to present their latest research and discuss key issues in language education. This series welcomes books on all areas of language teaching and learning, including but not limited to language education policy and politics, multilingualism, literacy, L1, L2, or foreign language acquisition, curriculum, classroom practice, pedagogy, teaching materials, and language teacher education and development. Books in the series are not limited to the discussion of the teaching and learning of English only.

Books in the series include:

The Acquisition of English Grammar and Phonology by Cantonese ESL Learners
Challenges, Causes and Pedagogical Insights
Alice Yin Wa Chan

Using Digital Portfolios to Develop Students' Writing
A Practical Guide for Language Teachers
Ricky Lam and Benjamin Luke Moorhouse

Enhancing Beginner-Level Foreign Language Education for Adult Learners
Language Instruction, Intercultural Competence, Technology, and Assessment
Edited by Ekaterina Nemtchinova

For more information about the series, please visit www.routledge.com/Routledge-Research-in-Language-Education/book-series/RRLE.

Using Digital Portfolios to Develop Students' Writing
A Practical Guide for Language Teachers

Ricky Lam and Benjamin Luke Moorhouse

LONDON AND NEW YORK

First published 2023
by Routledge
4 Park Square, Milton Park, Abingdon, Oxon OX14 4RN

and by Routledge
605 Third Avenue, New York, NY 10158

Routledge is an imprint of the Taylor & Francis Group, an informa business

© 2023 Ricky Lam and Benjamin Luke Moorhouse

The right of Ricky Lam and Benjamin Luke Moorhouse to be identified as authors of this work has been asserted in accordance with sections 77 and 78 of the Copyright, Designs and Patents Act 1988.

All rights reserved. No part of this book may be reprinted or reproduced or utilised in any form or by any electronic, mechanical, or other means, now known or hereafter invented, including photocopying and recording, or in any information storage or retrieval system, without permission in writing from the publishers.

Trademark notice: Product or corporate names may be trademarks or registered trademarks, and are used only for identification and explanation without intent to infringe.

British Library Cataloguing-in-Publication Data
A catalogue record for this book is available from the British Library

ISBN: 978-1-032-28240-4 (hbk)
ISBN: 978-1-032-28241-1 (pbk)
ISBN: 978-1-003-29586-0 (ebk)

DOI: 10.4324/9781003295860

Typeset in Times New Roman
by Apex CoVantage, LLC

I would like to extend my heartfelt thanks to my co-author Ben, who is always so collegial and inspiring. I also thank my research team, including Alli, Nancy, Gloria, Steve, and Ivan. With collective efforts, our team was able to overcome numerous challenges during the writing stage of this monograph. Last but not least, I am incredibly grateful to my wife Grace, who has supported me throughout my academic journey.

–Ricky

I wish to thank my co-author Ricky for inviting me to write this book with him. I have learnt so much from his guidance and support. I also wish to thank all the language teachers with whom I have had the privilege to work with and learn from. Their dedication and commitment are inspiring. Finally, I wish to thank my wife Yee Wan and children Brie and George. They make my personal and professional life so meaningful and rewarding.

–Ben

Contents

List of figures	ix
List of tables	x
Acknowledgements	xi
Glossary of terms	xii
Introduction	1
1 Background	3
2 Rationale for Digital Portfolios	10
3 Digital Portfolio-Based Curriculum	24
4 Digital Portfolios for Assessment	37
5 Feedback in Digital Portfolios	54
6 Digital Portfolio Application Tools	66
7 Vignette 1: Using Digital Portfolios to Facilitate Pre-School Learners' Literacy Development	86
8 Vignette 2: Adopting Digital Portfolios to Promote Primary School Learners' Self-Regulated Learning in Writing	100

Contents

9 Vignette 3: Blending Assessment and Learning of Writing in the Secondary School Language Classroom via Digital Portfolios   116

10 Future Directions   132

Useful Platforms, Apps, and Digital Tools   143
Index   146

Figures

1.1	Print Portfolio Processes	4
1.2	Digital Portfolio Processes	4
1.3	Evolution of Print and Digital Portfolios	6
2.1	Socio-Constructivist Approach	12
2.2	Features of Digital Portfolios	13
3.1	Design Framework of Digital Portfolio Curriculum	28
4.1	AFL–AAL–AOL Synergy	45
6.1	SAMR Model and Digital Portfolio Integration	71
7.1	Modelling Clay Letter Making	91
7.2	Letter Art	91
7.3	Letter, Word, or Sentence Jumble	92
8.1	Goal-setting Sheet	106
8.2	Sample Rubric for Fairy-Tale Stories	107
8.3	Example Genre Analysis Activity	109
9.1	Example Writing Task	122
9.2	Example Graphic Organiser	122
9.3	Example Graphic Organiser for Joint Construction	124
9.4	Example Co-Constructed Text	125

Tables

2.1	Types of Digital Portfolios	15
4.1	Classroom-Based Versus Standardised Digital Portfolio Assessment	40
4.2	Holistic Scoring Guide for Digital Portfolio	47
4.3	Primary Trait Rubrics for Digital Portfolio	48
4.4	Analytical Scoring Guide for Digital Portfolio	49
6.1	Lesson Plan	79

Acknowledgements

This work was funded by the Language Fund Under Research and Development Projects 2021–2022 of the Standing Committee on Language Education and Research (SCOLAR), Hong Kong SAR. The project reference number is (EDB(LE)/P&R/EL/203/12).

Glossary of terms

Introduction

Impromptu essay testing – a timed composition test, usually 1–1.5 hours where learners do not know the question and content of the test item in advance

Product-based instruction – an instructional approach where imitating, drilling, and rote-learning a model text are the key procedures

Self-regulated learning – learners engaging in goal-setting, monitoring, reflecting, and adjusting learning in relation to success criteria

Writing portfolios – a dossier where learners keep rough notes, early, interim, and final drafts, and related written homework assignments for the learning-oriented purpose

Chapter 1

Blogging tools – web-based platforms where learners can write and publish diary-like entries for peer comments

Compilation – a portfolio process where learners collect, manage, and organise their digital artefacts to fulfil the coursework requirement

Curation – a portfolio process where learners select, reflect, and showcase their representative digital artefacts to celebrate learning outcomes

Digital literacy – a learner's knowledge and skills to manage e-learning competently in a virtual environment

Inter-rater reliability – the consistency of evaluating the same piece of writing by two different raters

Learning management systems – interactive software or web-based tools which facilitate distance learning, remote instruction, synchronous chat, and asynchronous online learning, for example Moodle

Multimodal artefacts – evidence of learning presented in the form of texts, audios, videos, and graphics

Glossary of terms xiii

Process writing approach – a writing instructional approach which focuses on the process of writing, for example pre-writing, drafting, revising, editing, and publishing

Reflection – a portfolio process where learners monitor and review their learning metacognitively to make necessary adjustments

Chapter 2

Assessment for learning – using assessment information to support student learning as well as to improve writing instruction

Co-regulation of learning – learners regulate cognition, behaviours, and motivation together with peers and the teacher when learning writing

Digital identity – the role of learners as a writer (not a test-taker) and a portfolio creator when compiling their digital portfolios

Open-source tools – free digital tools which provide learners with a digital forum to share, publish, and disseminate their works, for example WordPress

Screencast written feedback – written feedback presented via a video clip that captures the teacher's verbal explanations and actual on-screen marking

Self-authoring software – software tools where learners can create, develop, and customise personalised web contents freely

Student response systems – online polling apps which enable teachers to include interactive or game-like elements in the lesson, for example Mentimeter

Socio-constructivism – new knowledge co-constructed by learners with their peers/teachers/parents and mostly mediated by the external environment, for example scaffolded input and linguistic exposure

Chapter 3

Product-based writing instruction – a didactic pedagogical approach emphasising rote-learning and imitation of the target text

Process-oriented writing instruction – an interactive pedagogical approach highlighting generative composing processes, such as brainstorming, drafting, and revising

Genre-based writing instruction – a communicative pedagogical approach underscoring the acquisition of specific genre features via the text deconstruction and co-construction procedures

Curriculum integration models – principles and strategies that guide teachers to integrate digital portfolio programmes into the existing curricula

Assessment rubrics – qualitative descriptions of multiple levels of competency for an assessment task alongside their respective letter grades or numerical scores

Practicality – the extent to which an assessment task or an assessment method is considered feasible among the teacher and students

English across the curriculum – English used as the medium of instruction in other content courses, such as science, mathematics, geography, and so on

Chapter 4

Assessment of learning – teacher evaluating student learning with marks or grades near the end of an instructional unit or a school term

Assessment as learning – a subset of assessment for learning, encouraging students to develop metacognitive capacity when learning writing

Digital portfolio assessment – utilising digital portfolios or the digital portfolio approach to assess student writing for grading and learning purposes

Scoring rubrics – a set of guidelines or principles linked with a performance scale or numerical scores which assists in evaluating student writing objectively

Holistic scoring method – aka impression marking, evaluating an entire digital portfolio comprehensively without focusing on a particular aspect

Primary trait scoring method – evaluating a digital portfolio by underscoring one key aspect, namely the ability to self-reflect with pertinent evidence

Analytic scoring method – evaluating a digital portfolio by emphasising several key aspects, namely content, interface, creativity, digital competence, and so on.

Chapter 5

E-feedback – online or offline assessment information generated by word processing software, AI-powered tools, or web-based automated feedback systems

Formative feedback – qualitative and descriptive feedback in the form of annotations/commentaries that help learners to improve digital composing

Summative feedback – quantitative and evaluative feedback in the form of letter grades, numerical scores, percentage, or grade point average to inform learners of their existing levels of competence

Feedback as a product – one-sided assessment information transmitted from the teacher to their learners

Feedback as a dialogue – assessment information considered as a dynamic conversation between the teacher and learners to enhance overall writing instruction

Feedback as an internal driver – feedback as a catalyst to assist learners to self-regulate their writing developments

Digital storytelling – learners mobilising multimedia artefacts to narrate a story, a critical moment, or a language learning experience to discover their identities

Chapter 6

Personalised learning – a learning approach which caters to learners' educational needs, preferences, and academic aptitudes within a negotiable language curriculum

Collaborative learning – a learning approach which supports social learning and peer learning through the task design, curriculum content, and assessment method

Cybersecurity – practices that protect computer systems, networks, and software from information leakage, online theft, and misuse of personalised data

Technology integration – the extent to which teachers incorporate education technology into their instructional approaches

Customised digital portfolio applications – software uniquely designed for supporting the digital portfolio processes, such as collection, curation, reflection, and publication

Chapter 7

Bottom-up processing skills – learners' acquisition of letter recognition, letter–sound relationship, and single-word meanings

Top-down processing skills – learners' acquisition of world language, language awareness, and genre structure

Literacy development – pre-school learners who acquire fundamental reading (shared reading) and writing (letter copying) skills in formal classroom settings

Chapter 8

Mini-lessons – short, targeted lessons that focus on a specific writing skill or genre feature

Publishing – the act of sharing a final draft of a piece of writing with its intended audience

Bring-your-own-device scheme (BYOD) – a school-based initiative where students are encouraged to bring a tablet or other Internet-enabled device to school for teaching and learning purposes

Chapter 9

eTwinning – an online classroom partnership formed between two or more groups of learners and prearranged by teachers

Public assessments – assessment tasks administered by government assessment agencies or recognised organisations that signify the end of a period of learning

High-stakes – an adjective used to describe assessments and examinations that can affect students' future educational and career opportunities

Exemplar – a text created or chosen by teachers to illustrate a specific genre or features of a genre

Performance analytics – computational analysis of test performance on digital tools to inform learners' strengths and weaknesses via simple statistics

Chapter 10

Authorial voice – opinions or stances as explicitly expressed by the author throughout a text

Self-efficacy belief – a psychological attribute where learners believe they can achieve certain goals with hard work, commitment, vision, and confidence

Flipped teaching – involving learners in preparing their online learning materials prior to the class and then having them perform problem-solving tasks with peers and the teacher in class

Digital divide – a demographic gap between those who have easy access to educational technology and those who do not

Audit culture – one form of quality assurance mechanism imposed externally by the district and the state to make school performance accountable to taxpayers

Doxxing – disclosing a person's individual data, such as age, address, occupation, income, or spouse online without getting the person's permission

Cyberstalking – following or chasing after a learner through electronic media (e.g. social media or e-learning platforms) with malevolent intention

Introduction

Writing portfolios have emerged in language teaching and assessment over the past three decades. Its electronic counterparts, digital portfolios, have been in the spotlight for two decades since the turn of the century. Despite their popularity and usefulness, teachers, language specialists, and researchers still want to know more about their pedagogical and evaluative values, given that portfolios are typically regarded as a "better" alternative to product-based instruction and impromptu essay testing (Yancey et al., 2015). Although there has been ample research examining the impacts of portfolios on student writing performances, these studies were mostly conducted in university contexts rather than in K-12 school settings (Nicolaidou, 2013). To this end, this monograph intends to fill this gap by equipping pre-service teachers, research postgraduate students, and teacher trainers with relevant knowledge and skills concerning the classroom application of digital portfolios in the K-12 writing classrooms.

The book underscores three unique features, which make it different from other portfolio-based scholarship. First, it seamlessly integrates principles, insights, and authentic examples to provide busy teachers with broadened perspectives when they try out digital portfolios in their own classrooms. Second, the volume includes a variety of learning-oriented tasks and up-to-date references, which increase readers' conceptual understanding and levels of confidence in using digital portfolios. The book can be used as a stand-alone reference or as an essential reading material in any teacher education/applied linguistics programme. Third, the book was written in a highly succinct manner with adequate elaborations, avoiding technical jargons and complicated linguistic structures, which may cause misconceptions. Taken together, these features empower prospective readers, particularly pre-service teachers, to readily innovate various types of digital portfolios.

DOI: 10.4324/9781003295860-1

The book has ten chapters and is broadly classified into four themes, namely (1) Rationale; (2) Curriculum and Assessment; (3) Application Tools; and (4) Vignettes. In Chapters 1 and 2, we unpack the background and theoretical rationale for adopting digital portfolios in the writing classrooms. In Chapters 3 and 4, we delineate how to incorporate the portfolio processes into the English writing curriculum and adopt digital portfolios as an assessment tool to evaluate and enhance student writing. In Chapters 5 and 6, we discuss the role of feedback in digital portfolios and its potential to promote self-regulated learning and autonomy and introduce common application tools to facilitate portfolio implementation. Chapters 7–9 describe three context-specific vignettes about the use of digital portfolios in pre-school, primary, and secondary school settings, respectively. Chapter 10 proposes the way forward for the future development of digital portfolios to promulgate effective writing instruction and assessment practices.

Each chapter ends with one of these four learning-focused tasks, including discussion tasks, mini-research tasks, self-evaluation tasks, or case studies. Discussion tasks consist of thought-provoking questions related to respective chapter content for consolidation. The questions can be used for self-study or for post-lecture assignment tasks. Classroom scenarios about the application of digital portfolios are used as prompts in mini-research tasks. These tasks are open-ended, harnessing readers' higher-order thinking and research skills. Self-evaluation tasks involve in-depth reflection upon why and how certain issues may arise when digital portfolios are implemented. Case studies encourage readers to make commentary on teacher experiences of utilising digital portfolios at various educational levels. These cases could serve as a model for those who plan to initiate a digital portfolio programme in their context. All in all, the aforementioned tasks enable readers to synthesise the learnt knowledge and their pedagogical repository.

References

Nicolaidou, I. (2013). E-portfolios supporting primary students' writing performance and peer feedback. *Computers & Education, 68*, 404–415.

Yancey, K. B., McElroy, S. J., & Powers, E. (2015). Composing, networks, and electronic portfolios: Notes toward a theory of assessing eportfolios. In H. A. McKee & D. N. DeVoss (Eds.), *Digital writing assessment and evaluation* (pp. 1–32). Utah State University Press.

1 Background

Definitions

Portfolios are broadly considered to be a dossier where students compile a range of print artefacts for both learning and grading purposes. More specifically, portfolios are defined as running records of students' efforts, growth, and achievements over time (Weigle, 2007). They serve as a companion to witness students' learning trajectories. The print portfolio processes feature *collection*, *selection*, and *reflection* within a feedback-rich environment, where learning writing simulates an interactive workshop mode (Yin, 2014). Collection refers to a systematic compilation of writing samples, such as interim and final drafts, handwritten notes, quizzes, homework assignments, and projects. Selection is a procedure where students purposefully choose either their representative or less-than-satisfactory works for a formative review. Reflection is a metacognitive process, wherein students self-evaluate the strengths and weaknesses of their writing development with opportunities for modifying works-in-progress (Curtis, 2018). Feedback-rich environments refer to a learning-supportive classroom, in which learning writing is at centre stage and multiple sources of feedback serve as catalysts to expedite students' learning. The print portfolio processes are illustrated in Figure 1.1.

The electronic version of portfolios is known as digital portfolios, which emphasise the creation of multimodal artefacts kept in a computer-based or web-based container. In writing, digital portfolios utilise software as an electronic folder, encouraging students to archive and curate digital multimodal compositions (e.g. audio, video, graphics, and texts) for showcasing their creativity, personality, and writing performance (Aygün & Aydin, 2016; Barrett, 2007). Likewise, the digital portfolio processes empower students to *create*, *evidence*, *connect*, and *reflect* upon artefacts for an alignment of curriculum, assessment, and learning goals (Yancey, 2009).

4 Background

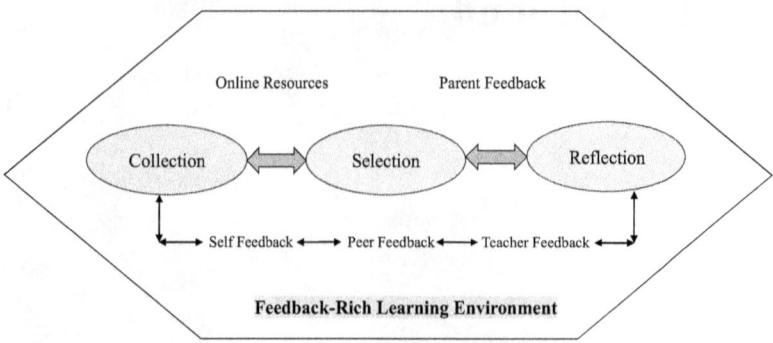

Figure 1.1 Print Portfolio Processes

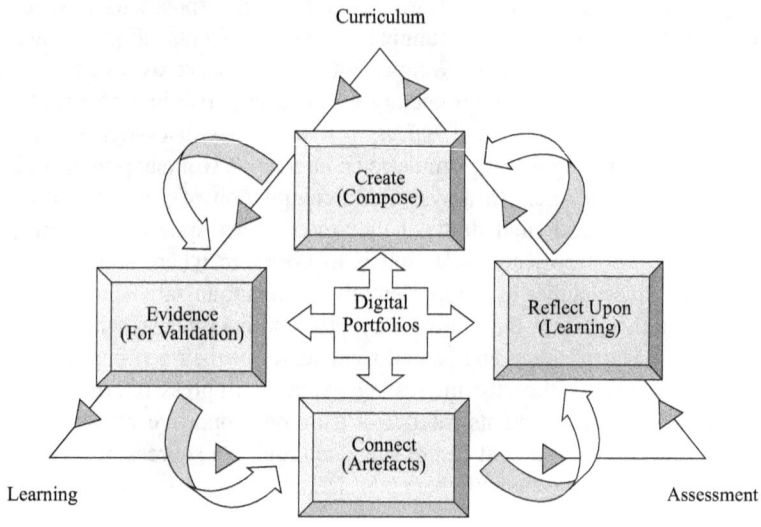

Figure 1.2 Digital Portfolio Processes

Creation is about how students compose a text electronically through multimedia software. Citing evidence refers to the use of pertinent artefacts to validate the achievements of target learning goals in a course/programme. Connection is to build hyperlinks and coherence of various artefacts to form a focused and digitised collection of works (Yancey, 2019). Reflection, similar to print portfolios, refers to a metacognitive review of learning progress in a writing programme or course. The digital portfolio processes are shown in Figure 1.2.

Applications

In primary/secondary school education, print portfolios are regarded as a learning companion for students who are mastering fundamental writing strategies (Jones, 2012). Parallel with the process writing approach, print portfolios facilitate students to draft, self-assess, peer assess, revise, and review their written works reflectively. The goal of print portfolio compiling is to enhance motivation, engagement, and autonomy in learning writing (Burner, 2014). While print portfolios are an effective and useful learning tool, digital portfolios can have greater utility, allowing students to showcase a range of learning artefacts other than written work. They may utilise out-of-class language learning (self-study), co-curricular activities (field trips), cross-disciplinary knowledge exchange (projects), and experiential learning (internships) as rich contexts to practice composing skills (Clark, 2010). These authentic experiences can be captured through weblogs, photos, video clips, audio-recording, social media posts, drawings, or links to relevant websites. The addition of hypertexts is thought to be pedagogically revealing to teachers and students (Kilbane & Milman, 2017). Also, digital portfolios can assist those who are linguistically (dyslexia), physically (visual impairment), and/or culturally (non-native speakers) disadvantaged in expressing their ideas via multimedia, such as audio texts or drawings. In other words, digital portfolios cater to learner diversity and promote inclusivity (McLaren, 2012).

Developments

Print portfolios originated in the 1970s, when they were adopted as a process-oriented instructional approach in L1 contexts. Towards the mid-1980s, a handful of U.S. universities started replacing exit writing exams with portfolios because the former had a high failure rate (Elbow & Belanoff, 1986). In the 1990s, portfolios were used in statewide reading and writing assessments. However, when piloted in two U.S. states, Pennsylvania and Kentucky, they were seen to be unsatisfactory due to a low inter-rater reliability (Koretz, 1998). Despite this, "the portfolio explosion" best described this era because a majority of K-16 teachers jumped on the portfolio bandwagon and implemented them in schools nationwide (Elbow & Belanoff, 1997). From the 2000s till now, the use of portfolios in the writing classroom has spread around the world in response to global curriculum reforms. Writing portfolios have become eclectic and context-specific to fulfil both learning and grading functions at the classroom level alongside high-stakes public exams (Hamp-Lyons, 2007).

Its electronic counterparts, digital portfolios, did not emerge in education until 1996 (Yancey, 1996). Between 1996 and 2000, the first generation

6 *Background*

of digital portfolios referred to print upload, meaning that students typed and saved their written work on desktops and then categorised them into respective computer-based folders (Yancey, 1996). From 2000 to 2010, the second-generation capitalised on the use of open-source learning systems, such as Mahara and Blackboard. Students could perform multiple functions on these systems, namely uploading, downloading, revising, annotating, and self-evaluating work (Butler, 2006; Yancey, 2004). Within this period, there were large-scale, digital portfolio implementations in L1 school settings, such as the REFLECT Initiative (Barrett, 2007) and ePEARL (Meyer et al., 2010). The subsequent decade of the 2010s, aka the third generation, witnessed widespread applications of common blogging tools (e.g. Wikis, WordPress, Google Sites) and social media sites (e.g. Facebook) as digital portfolio platforms (Karlin et al., 2016). Towards the end of the 2010s, there has been an advent of customised learning management

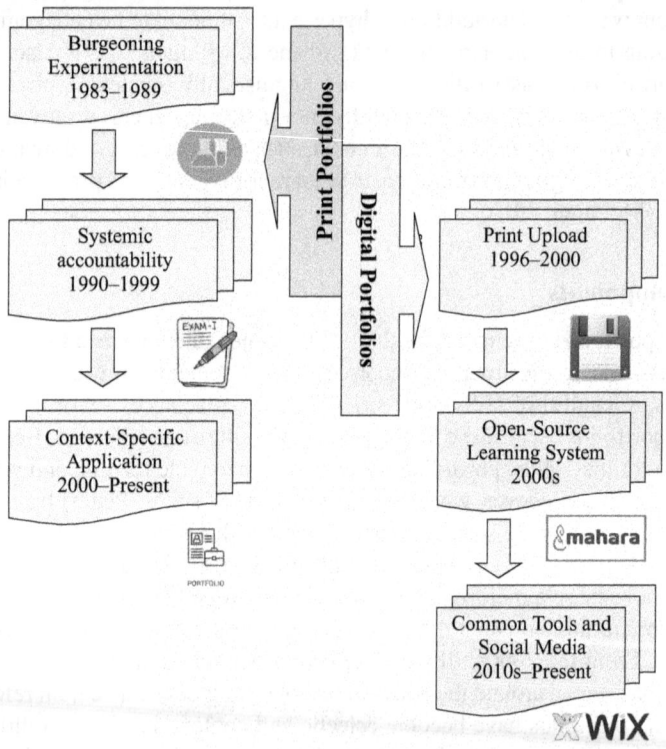

Figure 1.3 Evolution of Print and Digital Portfolios

systems, which cater to particular student demographics like Schoology, FreshGrade, Google Classroom, Edmodo, and Seesaw (Moorhouse, 2019). Of these, Google Classroom is the most common nowadays. The fourth generation is yet to come, but it will definitely emphasise wider connectivity, more sophisticated software, and full-blown development of digital literacies. A chronological development of print and digital portfolios is listed in Figure 1.3.

In writing, digital portfolios are beneficial to the development of self-regulated learning skills, because students are required to create, revise, curate, and reflect upon their written texts throughout the portfolio construction processes (Chang et al., 2016). Compilation and curation of artefacts to showcase learning appear to be the most important procedures, as these involve the active use of metacognitive thinking, technological competency, and self-regulated skills, which enable students to become lifelong learners in their future careers (Cicchino et al., 2019). To echo the ideas underpinning assessment for learning, the ability to plan, monitor, and review in digital environments should be promoted in writing pedagogy and curricula. In brief, digital portfolios, when applied in L2/EFL writing classrooms, have unlimited educational potentials although there remain caveats. The issues of privacy, confidentiality, and plagiarism become ongoing challenges for the foreseeable future.

Self-evaluation task

Fact check

Please tick "√" as appropriate.

		True	False
1	Print portfolios are more accessible than their digital counterparts.	☐	☐
2	Print and digital portfolios share common principles.	☐	☐
3	Marking a print portfolio is more challenging than marking an essay.	☐	☐
4	Print portfolios can be difficult to store.	☐	☐
5	Print portfolios were first used as an assessment tool in the 1970s.	☐	☐
6	Digital portfolios can support students with writing difficulties.	☐	☐
7	Print upload can be considered as one version of digital portfolios.	☐	☐
8	Digital portfolios are easier to implement than their print counterparts.	☐	☐

Preliminary survey

1. Do the principles of writing portfolios (e.g. learner-centredness) align with my educational philosophy? Why or why not?
2. Am I professionally ready to introduce digital portfolios in my future school?
3. If my answer to No. 2 is "yes", what motivates me to experiment with the use of the portfolios in my future school?
4. If my answer to No. 2 is "no", what inhibits me from trying out the use of portfolios in my future school?
5. What type of professional training and support do I want to receive and why do I want to have those training opportunities?
6. What possible limitations do I anticipate if I adopt digital portfolios in an EFL writing classroom?

Conclusion

The chapter has defined print and digital portfolios in language education and detailed their compilation processes, respectively. Then, the chapter has illustrated how these two broad types of portfolios were applied in the classroom context. After that, it has outlined a chronicle of print/digital portfolio evolution from the 1970s to the present. The chapter ends with a self-evaluation task with an aim to check on readers' understanding of print and digital portfolio applications.

References

Aygün, S., & Aydin, S. (2016). The use of e-portfolio in EFL writing: A review of literature. *ELT Research Journal*, *5*(3), 205–217.

Barrett, H. (2007). Researching electronic portfolios and learner engagement: The REFLECT initiative. *Journal of Adolescent & Adult Literacy*, *50*(6), 436–449.

Burner, T. (2014). The potential formative benefits of portfolio assessment in second and foreign language writing contexts: A review of the literature. *Studies in Educational Evaluation*, *43*, 139–149.

Butler, P. (2006). *A review of the literature on portfolios and electronic portfolios*. http://creativecommons.org/licenses/by-nc-sa/2.5/

Chang, C. C., Liang, C., Shu, K. M., Tseng, K. H., & Lin, C. Y. (2016). Does using e-portfolios for reflective writing enhance high school students' self-regulated learning? *Technology, Pedagogy and Education*, *25*(3), 317–336.

Cicchino, A., Efstathion, R., & Giarrusso, C. (2019). ePortfolio as curriculum: Revisualising the composition process. In K. B. Yancey (Ed.), *ePortfolio as curriculum: Models and practices for developing students' ePortfolio literacy* (pp. 13–32). Stylus Publishing.

Clark, J. E. (2010). The digital imperative: Making the case for a 21st-century pedagogy. *Computers and Composition, 27*, 27–35.

Curtis, A. (2018). Portfolios. In J. I. Liontas (Ed.), *The TESOL encyclopedia of English language teaching* (1st ed.). Wiley. https://doi.org/10.1002/9781118784235. eelt0326

Elbow, P., & Belanoff, P. (1986). Portfolios as a substitute for proficiency examinations. *College Composition and Communication, 37*(3), 336–339.

Elbow, P., & Belanoff, P. (1997). Reflections on an explosion: Portfolios in the 90s and beyond. In K. Yancey & I. Weiser (Eds.), *Situating portfolios: Four perspectives* (pp. 21–33). Utah State University Press.

Hamp-Lyons, L. (2007). The impact of testing practices on teaching: Ideologies and alternatives. In J. Cummins & C. Davison (Eds.), *International handbook of English language teaching* (pp. 487–504). Springer.

Jones, J. (2012). Portfolios as "learning companions" for children and a means to support and assess language learning in the primary school. *Education 3–13, 40*(4), 401–416.

Karlin, M., Ozogul, G., Miles, S., & Heide, S. (2016). The practical application of e-portfolios in K-12 classrooms: An exploration of three web 2.0 tools by three teachers. *TechTrends, 60*, 374–380.

Kilbane, C. R., & Milman, N. B. (2017). Examining the impact of the creation of digital portfolios by high school teachers and their students on teaching and learning. *International Journal of ePortfolio, 7*(1), 101–109.

Koretz, D. (1998). Large-scale portfolio assessment in the US: Evidence pertaining to the quality of measurement. *Assessment in Education: Principles, Policy & Practice, 5*(3), 309–334.

McLaren, S. V. (2012). Assessment is for learning: Supporting feedback. *International Journal of Technology and Design Education, 22*(2), 227–245.

Meyer, E., Abrami, P., Wade, C., Aslan, O., & Deault, L. (2010). Improving literacy and metacognition with electronic portfolios: Teaching and learning with ePEARL. *Computers & Education, 55*(1), 84–91.

Moorhouse, B. L. (2019). Seesaw: Https://web.seesaw.me. *RELC Journal, 50*(3), 493–496.

Weigle, S. C. (2007). Teaching writing teachers about assessment. *Journal of Second Language Writing, 16*(3), 194–209.

Yancey, K. B. (1996). The electronic portfolio: Shifting paradigms. *Computers and Composition, 13*, 259–262.

Yancey, K. B. (2004). Postmodernism, palimpsest, and portfolios: Theoretical issues in the representation of student work. *College Composition and Communication, 55*(4), 738–761.

Yancey, K. B. (2009). Electronic portfolios a decade into the twenty-first century: What we know, what we need to know. *Peer Review, 11*(1), 28–32.

Yancey, K. B. (Ed.). (2019). *ePortfolio as curriculum: Models and practices for developing students' ePortfolio literacy*. Stylus Publishing.

Yin, M. (2014). Portfolio assessment in the classroom. In A. J. Kunnan (Ed.), *The companion to language assessment* (Vol. II, pp. 659–676). Wiley.

2 Rationale for Digital Portfolios

Theoretical rationale for digital portfolios: socio-constructivism

Socio-constructivism is a major learning theory which draws from the highly influential work of Vygotsky. The theory suggests that learning is a socially mediated activity. The oft-cited principle of this theory is the zone of proximal development (ZPD). ZPD denotes that a student closes their learning gaps between the desired and existing academic performances through interactions with a more capable other, such as peers, parents, guardians, or teachers (Jones & Saville, 2016). Vygotsky (1978) pointed out that every child's learning development goes through two stages of interaction, first *between* people and then *inside* the child. Interaction with people and a wider environment is a core activity in the socio-constructivist approach to the teaching and learning of writing. Such interactivity of the ZPD constitutes the backbone of process-oriented, communal, and collaborative nature of digital portfolio design within which the relationship among teachers, students, and parents is strongly intertwined. Furthermore, active portfolio compilation may bring about renewed writer identities (not only restricted to sole-authorship), broader audience base (i.e. netizens on social media or other web-based tools), and alternative composing skills (management of multimodality in composition; Hafner, 2014; Pourdana & Tavassoli, 2022).

As to learning development occurring *inside* the child, they are expected to foster inner speech and thinking, which facilitate to bridge the learning gaps with an aid of more able counterparts. To put this intrapsychological aspect in a digital portfolio context, we consider it as a catalyst to support self-regulated learning, involving systematic coordination of the child's cognitive processes, motivational beliefs, and composing behaviours (Allal, 2021; Perrenoud, 1998). With that said, in a Vygotskian view, the

DOI: 10.4324/9781003295860-3

child's self-regulated learning is transitionally situated in the co-regulation of learning, where she remains dependent on a more capable other in the ZPD before she could independently manipulate the learnt composing skills (Allal, 2020). James (2017) added that within the ZPD, except for people, the child also interacts with her immediate environment, including pedagogical practices, curriculum contents, and societal expectations (i.e. achievements in high-stakes exams). Frequent interactions with the environment dovetail well with the rationale for digital portfolios, which highlight portability, connectivity, sustainability, and reflectivity as an authentic learning tool (Barrot, 2021). These digital portfolio attributes contribute to effective learning of writing because digital portfolios act as a catalyst for self- and co-regulation of learning in the classroom contexts (Bonner & Chen, 2019).

The child's inner speech and thinking typically refer to internal dialogues and reflective thinking, respectively. Socially mediated by tools, agents, artefacts, and language, internal dialogues empower the child's role in the learning and assessment processes, namely active participation in the design of portfolio contents (Dann, 2018). Similarly, reflective thinking promulgates metacognition in learning, such as metacognitive knowledge and metacognitive regulation when the child performs self-assessment to rework certain portfolio tasks and to manage digital portfolio keeping (Lam, 2015). Amid other ZPD aspects of socio-constructivism, reflective thinking is particularly relevant to average digital portfolio construction processes, where opportunities for self-reflection to develop student metacognitive capacity are always prioritised and takes centre stage (Tarrant & Holt, 2016). Despite the pedagogical value of reflective thinking, students may not necessarily internalise self-reflective skills independently even after exposure to scaffolded tasks. The ability of performing self-reflection in digital portfolio environments requires focused training, zealous commitments, repeated attempts, and moral support (Chang et al., 2016). To summarise, socio-constructivism characterises the ZPD, which explains a child's language development to happen on both social (interaction between people) and individual (inside themselves) levels. These two levels of interaction align with the uniqueness of digital portfolio processes – *social* connectivity (i.e. collegial alliance to nurture a community of practice) and *personalised* reflectivity (i.e. an individual pursuit of acquiring writing as craftsmanship). These two learning development levels are diagrammatically represented in Figure 2.1. The following section discusses the origin, features, types, and medium of classroom-based digital portfolios.

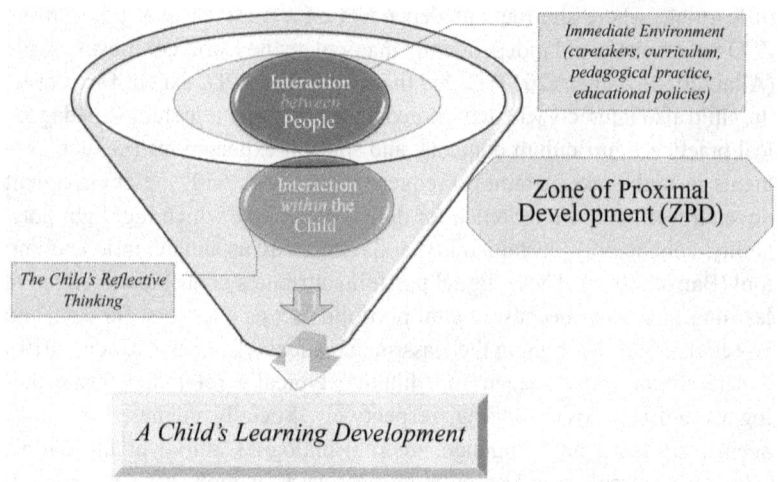

Figure 2.1 Socio-Constructivist Approach

Origin, features, types, and medium of digital portfolios

The "digital portfolio boom" in the late 1990s and early 2000s marked the origin of digital portfolios (Batson, 2002). The growing popularity of digital portfolios in language education can be explained by three phenomena over the past 25 years. First, the advent of the Internet and the World Wide Web in the early 1990s enabled computer users to connect around the globe. This technological advancement, alongside the emergence of numerous Web 2.0 tools (weblogs and social media), has facilitated the teaching and learning of writing (Eynon & Gambino, 2017). Second, entering the 2000s, Wi-Fi connectivity has become within the reach of hundreds of millions of people. This has allowed students to be able to use group and individual Internet-enabled devices in the classroom. Naturally, institutions at various educational levels, that is K-16, encourage teachers and students to migrate from print to digital portfolios. Meanwhile, such migration has alleviated some concerns when students manage their print portfolios, such as storage space, readership base, and ease of retrieval (Belgrad, 2013; Lam, 2021). Third, under the influence of global curriculum reforms (i.e. assessment for learning), digital portfolios have rapidly taken root in teachers' pedagogical repertoire and professional development goals (Aygün & Aydin, 2016; Burner, 2014). Their classroom applications are said to promote students' competencies in critical thinking, communication, collaboration, creativity, and media literacy, which are considered the most sought-after twenty-first-century skills for this fast-changing, increasingly A.I.-driven world (Kahn, 2014).

In general, digital portfolios have four common learning-oriented features. Being an alternative to the product-based pedagogical approach, digital portfolios are *learner-centred*, empowering students to construct new knowledge metacognitively by adopting self-regulated learning strategies, namely raising self-questions, practising "think-aloud", and self-revising while composing. Digital portfolios are *multimodal* by nature, since students are expected to collect audio, video, graphic, and textual artefacts when compiling their web-based portfolios or digital portfolios using open-source software. Digital portfolios also provide students with a *feedback-rich* environment so that self-, peer, teacher, and e-feedback will be readily created to inform effective L2 and EFL instruction. To allow reflection and validation, digital portfolios are normally *evidence-based*, where students mobilise a range of multimodal artefacts to corroborate how and the extent to which they have achieved certain learning goals critically (Barrett, 2007). The four digital portfolio features are summarised in Figure 2.2.

In the writing context, Yancey (2019, p. 236) has summarised six features of digital portfolios, including artefacts, a site of integration, curation, audience, reflection, and digital identity. (1) Artefacts, usually with reflection, provide a context and contents to construct a digital portfolio. (2) A site of integration is about adopting portfolios as a digital platform to narrativise students' learning trajectories from past, present, and to future. (3) Curation refers to the use of an array of learning evidence to document growth in writing and support achievements with reference to the set goals or external criteria usually stipulated by the district and the state. (4) Audience

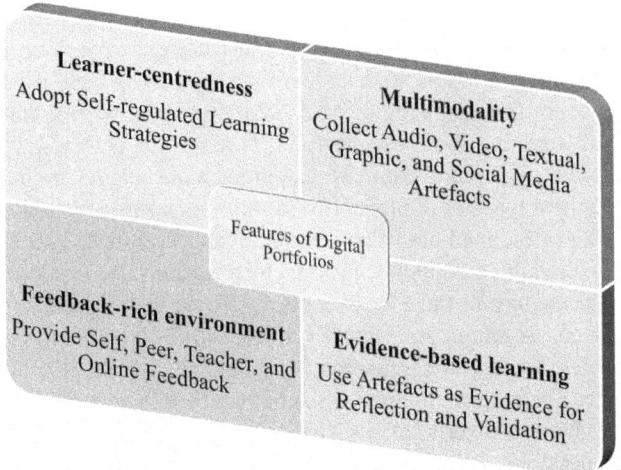

Figure 2.2 Features of Digital Portfolios

is chiefly peers, parents, teachers, or other outside members like writing scholars, professional raters, or university admission officers. (5) Reflection, according to Yancey, is a core activity, which separates coherent digital portfolios from haphazard information-giving websites. Reflective practice enables students to re-examine their artefacts introspectively and let them explicate how these works contribute to their learning outcomes. (6) Digital identity refers to the construction of a *learned* self as a proficient portfolio maker and her professional role in this writing journey. This digital identity is unique in every single portfolio and owned by the creator, students themselves, not the teacher.

In professional literature, there are three types of digital portfolios, including work, showcase, and assessment digital portfolios. Work portfolios tend to be collaborative, formative, and longitudinal, capturing a student's learning profile and their writing development over time. Their purpose is to document learning and provide the student with a virtual space to check on their own ongoing development. Showcase portfolios are normally individualised, summative, and short-lived by default, demonstrating a student's best ability with self-selected artefacts and reflective statements. Their purpose is to select the student's representative works and display her best potentials to internal and external stakeholders. Assessment portfolios are formal, evaluative, institution-led, and one-off in design, where a student is expected to submit prescribed coursework-based artefacts for grading near the end of an instructional unit or an academic programme. Their purpose is to facilitate the student to fulfil graduation, admission, or licensure requirements, such as in nursing and teacher education contexts. Despite their distinctive attributes and purposes, the three types of digital portfolios are not as clear-cut as we anticipate, especially when teachers apply them in the writing classrooms. For instance either work or showcase portfolio is used to assess students' writing abilities as well, especially if both digital portfolio pedagogies are parts of the school writing curriculum. A blend of work and showcase portfolios is somewhat common, given that teachers tend to monitor the process and product of student learning holistically. The three types of digital portfolios are summarised in Table 2.1.

Speaking of the medium of presenting digital portfolios, Yancey (2004) has categorised three digital media, on which teachers can introduce digital portfolio pedagogy in their work contexts. These media include (1) print uploaded; (2) an online assessment system; and (3) web-based portfolios. Print uploaded refers to a transition from a student's print portfolio into a digital one. The student simply types and saves their print works into digital files (e.g. Word, PowerPoint, JPEG, and/or PDF files) and uploads them to iPads, desktops, laptops, or Google Drive. This medium is particularly

Table 2.1 Types of Digital Portfolios

	Type of Digital Portfolios		
	Work	Showcase	Assessment
Attribute	Collaborative and longitudinal	Individualised and short-lived	Institution-led and formal
Uniqueness	Tracking student writing development	Showcasing student best potential	Fulfilling externally imposed requirements
Purpose	Formative	Summative	Evaluative
Application	Used as a learning companion to document growth	Used as a platform to display student representative works	Used as testimony for graduation, university admission, or scholarship application

suitable for those students who are new to the portfolio pedagogy and are adjusting their momentum when only instructional materials are switched to the digital mode. It is considered the easiest start-up for students who have limited computer skills.

An online assessment system refers to a commercially or institutionally designed platform, where a student uploads, stores, and organises preselected learning artefacts for both learning and grading purposes. Despite its storage and content management functions, these online assessment systems are likely to downplay the role of reflection in the student's portfolio journey. Furthermore, these systems usually accommodate other services, namely advising tools, institutional portals, and programme record management (Kimball, 2005). Yancey (2004, p. 745) has warned that an online assessment system is very "un-portfolio-like" because the student has to comply with the system's configuration strictly without much flexibility. Web-based portfolios are about the use of open-source tools (WordPress) or self-authoring software (Wix) to create customised digital portfolios by adding URLs, video clips, podcasts, galleries, and social media links to the suites. The benefit of this medium assists a student to create multimedia and hypertextual artefacts at her fingertips although she needs to be I.T. savvy. The student also enjoys full autonomy for designing a personalised digital portfolio template to document her writing development. The subsequent section reports a brief literature review by looking into the pros and cons of digital portfolios and their effectiveness.

Review of literature

Pros and cons

Digital portfolios, adopted at the classroom level, have several advantages. They facilitate teaching and learning of writing. First, digital portfolios allow teachers to adopt an *inductive, dynamic* approach to teaching writing. The practice of multi-drafting, self- and peer assessment, and self-reflection becomes pedagogically workable on digital platforms because students take up active agency and responsibility when doing various portfolio tasks inside and outside the classroom (Butler, 2006; Nicol et al., 2019). Precious contact hours may reserve for in-class online interactions (via student response systems, e.g. Mentimeter) and essential face-to-face teaching of specific written genres and composing strategies (Moorhouse & Kohnke, 2020). Second, through innovative software, teachers can provide students with diverse forms of feedback more efficiently, namely online written feedback (e.g. e-Rater www.ets.org/erater), annotated PDFs, audio files (e.g. Audacity www.audacityteam.org/), and screencast written feedback (e.g. Jing aka Snagit, www.techsmith.com/screen-capture.html). With these, students immerse themselves in a feedback-rich environment to improve composing and metacognitive skills (Lee, 2017). Third, digital portfolios, other than a storage space, promote evidence-based learning because students can use hyperlinks/texts, voiced-over PowerPoint, self-authoring websites, or digital videos on streaming media to create multimodal evidence for showcasing their learning trajectories (Lam, 2021; Yancey, 2019).

Despite their benefits, digital portfolios have noticeable barriers, namely computer literacy, accessibility to infrastructure, and constant change in technology. If digital portfolios are widely applied in school, teachers and students are to be computer literate and get used to manipulating the interface of various digital tools (Cho, 2018). However, not every teacher or student is proficient in managing digital portfolios and has received respective training. Regarding the implementation, the levels of teachers' and students' *computer literacy* obviously come into play (Clancy & Gardner, 2017). *Accessibility* to digital gadgets and Wi-Fi connection appears to be another hurdle. Unless schools provide students with a tablet, teachers cannot assume that students can afford to own one, especially those socioeconomically disadvantaged students. Having stable Wi-Fi connection with sufficient mobile data within school premises and/or at home is essential if students are required to complete portfolio tasks, like uploading, downloading, or creating video files (Siu, 2013). Digital software tools and learning management systems come and go, so that teachers and students need to keep abreast of *technological* advancement. Without constantly updating their skills, teachers and students perhaps find it taxing to use those tools to improve teaching and the learning of writing (Beach, 2012).

Effectiveness of digital portfolios

In research, print portfolios tend to motivate students to produce more and better written texts than being taught by the product-based writing instruction (Lam & Lee, 2010). Digital portfolios are claimed to make students more motivated when they engage in the portfolio compilation processes. Students are given more autonomy to collect, select, and reflect upon their written works. Through this newly acquired independence, they develop ownership and a sense of achievement in learning writing. It was reported that students generally fostered a positive attitude towards writing when they fully engaged in digital portfolio tasks, such as creating, curating, evidencing, and publishing their multimodal compositions online (Lam, 2019). For instance, in Aygün and Aydin's (2016) review study, they categorised that digital portfolios could enhance writing motivation due to the fact that students could develop their writers' identities more readily through a wide range of multimedia tools, such as weblogs, Wikis, digital videos, and social media networks (e.g. Facebook or Instagram). In her four-month action research study conducted in Greece, Daskalogiannaki (2012) found that when 12 eighth graders created their "blogfolios" (i.e. weblog-based portfolios), they became much more motivated to compose longer texts with greater complexity than before.

Al-Qallaf and Al-Mutairi (2016) investigated how 23 Grade 5 Kuwaiti students responded to a weblog-based portfolio programme. The findings showed that the participants made fewer grammatical errors and became more motivated and independent in composing. Moreover, they displayed a more positive learning disposition when it came to learning English as a foreign language. In their study, Cheng and Chau (2009) reported that 15 post-secondary school students were motivated to perform self-reflection through videos within a context of digital portfolios. Regardless of this encouraging evidence, in a study exploring the relationship between motivation for composing digital portfolios and reflection among 156 Grade 11 students, De Bruin et al. (2012) found out that only one-fifth of the paragraphs in 37 portfolios consisted of reflection. Among these tasks, only 0.8% of the paragraphs involved deep reflection. The authors emphasised that motivation for composing a portfolio was fair, which was unrelated to the overall quality of reflection in the students' portfolios. Likewise, in a questionnaire study with 419 Grades 4–6 students in the Netherlands, Baas et al. (2020) found that compiling a portfolio may not necessarily enhance student motivation for writing. Instead, the participants felt that assessment for learning practices motivated their learning. With these less promising outcomes in mind, when teachers attempt the portfolio approach, they may consider harnessing the learning-oriented potentials of digital portfolios more strategically to increase student motivation for writing.

Except writing motivation, digital portfolios are said to support student development of metacognitive skills when composing, namely self-reflection. Meanwhile, this reflective thinking has a close connection with text improvement. Sun (2010) investigated how 23 undergraduate students composed their weblog entries within a digital portfolio environment in one academic writing course. The results illustrated that the participants had marked improvement in the last three entries as compared to the first three. They were found to develop better monitoring skills and learner autonomy after the study. Meyer et al. (2010) conducted a digital portfolio study in three Canadian provinces involving 296 Grades 4–6 students. Adopting a non-equivalent pre-test–post-test design, the researchers examined whether the students, after using ePEARL – a digital portfolio tool, had improvements in their writing performances and composing skills. The outcomes confirmed that the students had a marked increase in their composition scores and became more self-regulated in learning writing. In their questionnaire study administered with 26 undergraduate students, Cheng and Chau (2013) explored the relationship between students' self-regulated ability and digital portfolio scores. The findings showed that the regular use of cognitive (elaborating and critical thinking), metacognitive (monitoring and reflecting), and collaborative learning strategies enabled students to attain higher numerical scores in their digital portfolios.

Moreover, digital portfolios can help students improve their writing across drafts and other composing skills. Nicolaidou (2010) implemented a weblog as student digital portfolios among three groups of Grade 4 students. She found that the students' writing improved from the first to third drafts and then from the sixth to eighth drafts in their portfolios. Aydin (2014) investigated 101 EFL university freshmen's perceptions and attitudes about using Facebook as a tool for portfolio keeping. The findings revealed that other than improved literacy skills, the participants enhanced their research skills while constructing their Facebook-based portfolios. In another study, Nicolaidou (2013) introduced "process" digital portfolios with the component of peer feedback in one Grade 4 class. After the study, the 20 informants improved their writing and peer feedback skills. They could identify their peers' errors more accurately and give direct/indirect feedback to their peers over time although only average- and high-ability students benefitted more from the portfolio implementation. While digital portfolios are generally conducive to learning gains in writing, they do not necessarily enhance reflective thinking skills. Händel et al. (2020) revealed that students using portfolios outperformed their non-portfolio peers in the exam performances, but they showed no progress in their extensive use of self-regulated learning skills. Yancey (2015) has also claimed that scoring digital portfolios with rubrics was not sufficient. Instead, having conversations with students emphasising reflective thinking could help students improve future learning.

Drawing from the aforementioned review, digital portfolios are somewhat effective in enhancing writing motivation, metacognitive composing skills, and writing performances, depending on the extent to which students are involved in the portfolio programme as well as how much academic support they get from the teachers, peers, and parents. The next section is a discussion task, which gives details of how to set up a digital writing portfolio programme.

Discussion task

a   Study and discuss the following questions:

1   Which feature of digital portfolios do you think has aligned with your educational philosophy? How does this feature enable you to adopt digital portfolios as a pedagogical approach?

2   Which type of digital portfolios could promote assessment for learning in L2/EFL writing? (*Assessment for learning is defined as an effective pedagogical approach that informs teachers and students of how they can continue to improve teaching and learning respectively through constructive assessment data generated during the lesson time and/or from classroom assessment tasks.* For details, please refer to Chapter 4.)

3   Among Yancey's (2004) three types of digital medium, which one is the most suitable for your learners if you are about to start a digital portfolio programme? Why?

4   Identify ONE disadvantage of digital portfolios which you are likely to encounter when introducing the approach in your work context. Please elaborate on your response.

b   When teachers plan to set up a digital portfolio programme in their classrooms, they may observe these four considerations. They include (1) teachers' and students' computer literacy; (2) nature of the teaching context (process-oriented vs. product-oriented writing instruction); (3) purpose of digital portfolios (formative or summative); and (4) content organisation of digital portfolios (Al Kahtani, 1999). Think about and answer the following questions:

1. Among the four considerations, which one is the most necessary to tackle if teachers aspire to create a digital portfolio programme successfully and why?
2. How do teachers resolve the point (2) – nature of the teaching context when digital portfolios are applied in a product-oriented writing classroom where multiple drafting is not practised?
3. Give TWO suggestions in which teachers can assist students to manage their portfolio contents more methodically. (*Hints: choice of various web-authoring tools or common portfolio software.*)

Conclusion

The chapter first unveiled the theoretical rationale for digital portfolios, namely socio-constructivism. It then discussed the origin, features, types, and medium of digital portfolios in the L2/EFL classroom context. The chapter further reviewed current literature with a focus on the pros and cons of digital portfolios and their effectiveness in terms of writing motivation, metacognitive composing skills, and learning gains. Finally, the chapter ended with a discussion task, which invited readers to evaluate the four considerations if they want to introduce a digital portfolio programme in their workplaces successfully.

References

Allal, L. (2020). Assessment and the co-regulation of learning in the classroom. *Assessment in Education: Principles, Policy & Practice, 27*(4), 332–349.

Allal, L. (2021). Involving primary school students in the co-construction of formative assessment in support of writing. *Assessment in Education: Principles, Policy & Practice, 28*(5–6), 584–601.

Al Kahtani, S. (1999). Electronic portfolios in ESL writing: An alternative approach. *Computer Assisted Language Learning, 12*(3), 261–268.

Al-Qallaf, C. L., & Al-Mutairi, A. S. R. (2016). Digital literacy and digital content supports learning: The impact of blogs on teaching English as a foreign language. *The Electronic Library, 34*(3), 522–547.

Aydin, S. (2014). EFL writers' attitudes and perceptions toward e-portfolio use. *TechTrends, 58*(2), 59–77.

Aygün, S., & Aydin, S. (2016). The use of e-portfolio in EFL writing: A review of literature. *ELT Research Journal, 5*(3), 205–217.

Baas, D., Vermeulen, M., Castelijns, J., Martens, R., & Segers, M. (2020). Portfolios as a tool for AfL and student motivation: Are they related? *Assessment in Education: Principles, Policy & Practice, 27*(4), 444–462.

Rationale for Digital Portfolios 21

Barrett, H. C. (2007). Researching electronic portfolios and learner engagement: The REFLECT initiative. *Journal of Adolescent & Adult Literacy, 50*(6), 436–449.

Barrot, J. S. (2021). Effects of Facebook-based e-portfolio on ESL learners' writing performance. *Language, Culture and Curriculum, 34*(1), 95–111.

Batson, T. (2002). The electronic portfolio boom: What's it all about? *Syllabus, 16*(5). www.syllabus.com/article.asp?id=6984

Beach, R. (2012). Uses of digital tools and literacies in the English language arts classroom. *Research in the Schools, 19*(1), 45–59.

Belgrad, S. F. (2013). Portfolios and e-portfolios: Student reflection, self-assessment, and global setting in the learning process. In J. H. McMillan (Ed.), *Sage handbook of research on classroom assessment* (pp. 331–346). Sage.

Bonner, S. M., & Chen, P. P. (2019). *Systematic classroom assessment: An approach for learning and self-regulation.* Routledge.

Burner, T. (2014). The potential formative benefits of portfolio assessment in second and foreign language writing contexts: A review of the literature. *Studies in Educational Evaluation, 43*, 139–149.

Butler, P. (2006). *A review of the literature on portfolios and electronic portfolios.* http://creativecommons.org/licenses/by-nc-sa/2.5/

Chang, C. C., Liang, C., Shu, K. M., Tseng, K. H., & Lin, C. Y. (2016). Does using e-portfolios for reflective writing enhance high school students' self-regulated learning? *Technology, Pedagogy and Education, 25*(3), 317–336.

Cheng, G., & Chau, J. (2009). Digital video for fostering self-reflection in an e-portfolio environment. *Learning, Media and Technology, 34*(4), 337–350.

Cheng, G., & Chau, J. (2013). Exploring the relationship between students' self-regulated learning ability and their e-portfolio achievement. *The Internet and Higher Education, 17*(1), 9–15.

Cho, H. (2018). The pitfalls and promises of electronic portfolio assessment with secondary English language learners. In J. Perren, K. B. Kelch, J. Byun, S. Cervantes, & S. Safari (Eds.), *Applications of CALL theory in ESL and EFL environments* (pp. 111–129). IGI Global.

Clancy, M., & Gardner, J. (2017). Using digital portfolios to develop non-traditional domains in special education settings. *International Journal of ePortfolio, 7*(1), 93–100.

Dann, R. (2018). *Developing feedback for pupil learning.* Routledge.

Daskalogiannaki, E. (2012). Developing and assessing EFL students' writing skills via a class-blog. *Research Papers in Language Teaching and Learning, 3*(1), 269–292.

De Bruin, H. L., van der Schaaf, M. F., Oosterbaan, A. E., & Prins, F. J. (2012). Secondary-school students' motivation for portfolio reflection. *Irish Educational Studies, 31*(4), 415–431.

Eynon, B., & Gambino, L. M. (2017). *High-impact ePortfolio practice: A catalyst for student, faculty, and institutional learning.* Stylus Publishing.

Hafner, C. A. (2014). Embedding digital literacies in English language teaching: Students' digital video projects as multimodal ensembles. *TESOL Quarterly, 48*(4), 655–685.

Händel, M., Wimmer, B., & Ziegler, A. (2020). E-portfolio use and its effects on exam performance – a field study. *Studies in Higher Education, 45*(2), 258–270.

James, M. (2017). (Re)viewing assessment: Changing lenses to refocus on learning. *Assessment in Education: Principles, Policy & Practice*, *24*(3), 404–414.

Jones, N., & Saville, N. (2016). *Learning oriented assessment: A systemic approach*. Cambridge University Press.

Kahn, S. (2014). E-portfolios: A look at where we've been, where we are now, and where we're (possibly) going. *Peer Review*, *16*(1). www.aacu.org/publications-research/periodicals/e-portfolios-look-where-weve-been-where-we-are-now-and-where-were

Kimball, M. (2005). Database e-portfolio systems: A critical appraisal. *Computers and Composition*, *22*(4), 434–458.

Lam, R. (2015). Understanding EFL students' development of self-regulated learning in a process-oriented writing course. *TESOL Journal*, *6*(3), 527–553.

Lam, R. (2019). *Using portfolios in language teaching*. RELC New Portfolio Series 4. SEAMEO Regional Language Centre.

Lam, R. (2021). Using e-portfolios to promote assessment of, for, as learning in EFL writing. *The European Journal of Applied Linguistics and TEFL*, *10*(1), 101–120.

Lam, R., & Lee, I. (2010). Balancing the dual functions of portfolio assessment. *ELT Journal*, *64*(1), 54–64.

Lee, I. (2017). *Classroom writing assessment and feedback in L2 school contexts*. Springer.

Meyer, E., Abrami, P., Wade, C., Aslan, O., & Deault, L. (2010). Improving literacy and metacognition with electronic portfolios: Teaching and learning with ePEARL. *Computers & Education*, *55*(1), 84–91.

Moorhouse, B. L., & Kohnke, L. (2020). Using Mentimeter to elicit student responses in the EAP/ESP classroom. *RELC Journal*, *51*(1), 198–204.

Nicol, D., Serbati, A., & Tracchi, M. (2019). Competence development and portfolios: Promoting reflection through peer review. *AISHE-J*, *11*(2), 1–13.

Nicolaidou, I. (2010). Using a weblog as an ePortfolio tool in elementary school essay writing [Conference paper]. In P. Escudeiro (Ed.), *9th European conference on e-learning* (pp. 417–426). Instituto Superior de Engenharia de Porto.

Nicolaidou, I. (2013). E-portfolios supporting primary students' writing performance and peer feedback. *Computers & Education*, *68*, 404–415.

Perrenoud, P. (1998). From formative evaluation to a controlled regulation of learning processes: Towards a wider conceptual field. *Assessment in Education: Principles, Policy & Practice*, *5*(1), 85–102.

Pourdana, N., & Tavassoli, K. (2022). Differential impacts of e-portfolio assessment on language learners' engagement modes and genre-based writing improvement. *Language Testing in Asia*, *12*(7). https://doi.org/10.1186/s40468-022-00156-7

Siu, F. (2013). The incorporation of ePortfolios into five EFL courses – barriers encountered in the diffusion of technology. *Journal of Interactive Learning Research*, *24*(2), 211–231.

Sun, Y. C. (2010). Extensive writing in foreign-language classrooms: A blogging approach. *Innovations in Education and Teaching International*, *47*(3), 327–339.

Tarrant, P., & Holt, D. (2016). *Metacognition in the primary classroom*. Routledge.

Vygotsky, L. (1978). *Mind in society: The development of higher psychological processes*. Harvard University Press.

Yancey, K. B. (2004). Postmodernism, palimpsest, and portfolios: Theoretical issues in the representation of student work. *College Composition and Communication*, 55(4), 738–761.

Yancey, K. B. (2015). Grading ePortfolios: Tracing two approaches, their advantages, and their disadvantages. *Theory into Practice*, 54(4), 301–308.

Yancey, K. B. (Ed.). (2019). *ePortfolio as curriculum: Models and practices for developing students' ePortfolio literacy*. Stylus Publishing.

3 Digital Portfolio-Based Curriculum

Context of writing instruction

Writing instruction is a key aspect of language teaching, in addition to the teaching of reading, listening, speaking, grammar, and vocabulary. It is usually considered the most challenging aspect to teach because student mastery of writing involves a complex interplay of linguistic, semantic, communicative, and pragmatic competence in the language system to enable them to utilise different genres to achieve purposeful communications (Lam, 2015). In school settings, writing is taught together with other sub-skills, namely reading, to nurture students' literacy skills. Thus, writing is regarded as an integrative skill rather than a separate language skill. Engaging students to write after intensive or extensive reading becomes an integral part of writing instruction, for instance readers' responses, reflective journals, text appreciation pieces, and reports (Lee, 2017).

In language teaching, there are three major approaches to writing instruction, namely product-oriented, process-oriented, and genre-based approaches. The product-oriented approach emphasises the products of writing, say the final drafts, neglecting how a text is composed. Teachers adopting the product-oriented approach generally provide a model text and instruct students to create a similar text with different content (Badge & White, 2000). This approach underscores mastery of text production rather than the author's writing experience. It promotes accuracy and text imitation. The approach is conceptually grounded in the theory of behaviourism. In contrast, the process-oriented approach highlights the process of writing, namely the author's evolving writing development. This approach advocates generative writing skills like brainstorming, drafting, editing, and revising. Teachers utilising the process-oriented approach usually dedicate instructional time to each stage of the writing process, guiding students to construct a complete text over a number of lessons (Badge & White, 2000).

DOI: 10.4324/9781003295860-4

It shifts the focus from the text to the author who is deemed to be creative and expressive. The process approach is grounded in the theory of constructivism (Li, 2017). The genre-based approach encourages students to master lexico-grammatical features and schematic structures of individual genres to fulfil their social functions. This approach prepares students to participate in various discourse communities competently. The teacher and students will analyse the content, organisational structure, and language of various genres, engage in text co-construction, and write texts with social purpose and audience in mind (Badge & White, 2000). It focuses on the interconnectedness between the text, its context, and the audience. The approach is rooted in the systemic functional linguistics model (Hyland, 2016).

In Hong Kong, the Education Bureau has promoted process-oriented and genre-based approaches to writing for over two decades. Since 2009, the language arts components have been formally incorporated into the English language curriculum (Grades 1–12), so that students have ample opportunities to learn how to compose poems, lyrics, short stories, and drama scripts with the process-oriented approach (Curriculum Development Council, 2017). Despite the government's curriculum reform initiatives, a majority of teachers still adopt the product-oriented approach (Lee, 2021). Often, teachers expressed concerns that they had no time to try out process-oriented or genre-based approaches, as they have to prioritise preparing students for the school and public assessments (Lam, 2018a). Second, they reported being overwhelmed with heavy marking loads (Lee & Coniam, 2013). Third, some teachers suggested that they lacked adequate training in attempting the process-oriented and genre-based approaches because they found it difficult to teach students how to compose a full-length text with technical terms (Lee et al., 2016). Similar findings have been found in other international contexts. Apparently, there are a plethora of individual, institutional, and contextual barriers when teachers innovated alternative instructional and assessment practices (Gan & Leung, 2020). Against this backdrop, we illustrate how teachers could integrate digital portfolio components in the three writing instruction scenarios more successfully.

Integration into curriculum

Prior to the discussion on curriculum integration, we discuss four differences between the traditional English language curriculum and digital portfolio-based curriculum in terms of students' and teachers' roles, objectives, content, and assessment. First, in the traditional curriculum, teachers play the role of a language expert, whereas students assume the role of a passive learner. In digital portfolio classrooms, teachers and students enjoy equal status to co-construct new knowledge through the portfolio compilation process, namely collection, curation, reflection, and publication (Lam, 2017). Second, the objectives of the traditional English language curriculum are prescriptive and restricted by a scheme of work stipulated by teachers and department chairs. Concerning the objectives of the digital portfolio-based curriculum, they are open-ended, descriptive, and negotiable because the portfolio approach characterises inclusivity, flexibility, and transparency (Burner, 2014). Third, the traditional curriculum tends to be grammar-focused and exam-driven, which are somewhat contrived and less useful to students' actual learning needs. However, a curriculum with digital portfolio components entails up-to-date knowledge (current topical issues), practical language skills (uptake of colloquial English), and authentic instructional materials (strategic use of multimodal artefacts) connecting with the external world. Fourth, the digital portfolio-based curriculum aligns pedagogy and assessment positively, since digital portfolios emphasise self-reflection, which makes writing instruction and assessment integrative and sustainable (Light et al., 2012). In the traditional curriculum, teaching and assessment of writing remain disconnected.

To integrate digital portfolio elements into the existing English language curriculum, there are three possible approaches, including parallel, blended, and separated models (cf. Lam, 2019). As to the parallel model, the portfolio programme is an add-on component to the mainstream curriculum rather than an integral part. The plus side of this model is that digital portfolios could be introduced at any time or in any teaching unit the teacher deems appropriate. After all, this model promotes flexibility in application and diversity in displaying learning artefacts. Depending on the scope and breadth of the programme, the teacher may require students to include one teaching unit, say four weeks of written works, for example quizzes, drafts, mind maps in their digital portfolios for peer review and self-reflection. The teacher could also invite students to showcase their best works in multimodal formats at the end of the school year, such as podcasts, audio reflection, and video clips (amateur documentaries). The parallel model is particularly suitable for the product-based/exam-oriented writing classrooms, where process writing, peer assessment, self-reflection, and compilation of evidence are not regular features.

Regarding the blended model, the portfolio programme is said to be partially or fully integrated into the English language curriculum. In other words, the digital portfolio approach is also a default instructional approach. Other than using digital portfolios as homework assignment containers, the teacher can use this digital platform, namely e-Class (an intranet system widely used in Hong Kong schools), Google Classroom, Moodle, or Padlet to facilitate flipped learning and synchronous remote teaching. In this

Digital Portfolio-Based Curriculum 27

model, digital portfolios are a built-in component that empowers students to be autonomous, creative, metacognitive, and computer literate when they actively engage in various portfolio learning tasks. The blended model dovetails nicely with process-oriented writing classrooms, as the organic nature of writing is encapsulated in digital portfolio-based classrooms. Regardless of the merits of this model, teachers need to plan how many professional hours are allocated to the actual implementation of portfolio-based writing instruction. It is important to remember that managing digital portfolios for teaching and learning of writing is time-consuming. It requires time to be allocated for training, monitoring, and evaluating the portfolio programme along with other non-teaching duties.

As regards the separated model, it is somewhat unique, because it belongs neither to the parallel nor to the blended models. This model views the digital portfolio experience as personalised. It is private, formative, and learning-oriented and does not link to any summative evaluations. Within this model, digital portfolios are likened to students' learning companions, which help them keep track of their writing trajectories across grade levels and beyond graduation. The advantages of this model include confidentiality and ownership, as students can protect their privacy when performing digital self-reflection and exercise their agency to develop a digital portfolio of their own. Students can build up their learner identities by way of self-authorship naturally (Light et al., 2012). Nonetheless, the minus side is that teachers may find it taxing to monitor students' progress regularly, especially when this model is voluntary. Students are expected to be self-disciplined, committed, and conscientious about their portfolio management routines over an extensive period of time. This model suits all three approaches of writing instruction. With that said, students may find it productive to take stock of multiple genres they have composed over time via a genre-based curriculum and self-assess what they have achieved and what they need to improve independently. No matter which model of curriculum integration teachers adopt, they should consider their educational philosophies, instructional approaches, students' aptitudes, students' learning styles and needs, and school culture. The following section reveals how teachers can design a school-based digital portfolio-based programme with a validated design framework.

Design framework

The curriculum design framework discussed here was first published in Lam's (2018a) monograph, which provided a user-friendly guide for teachers to create and set up their print portfolio-based programmes (Figure 3.1). It was developed, revised, and consolidated based upon a validation

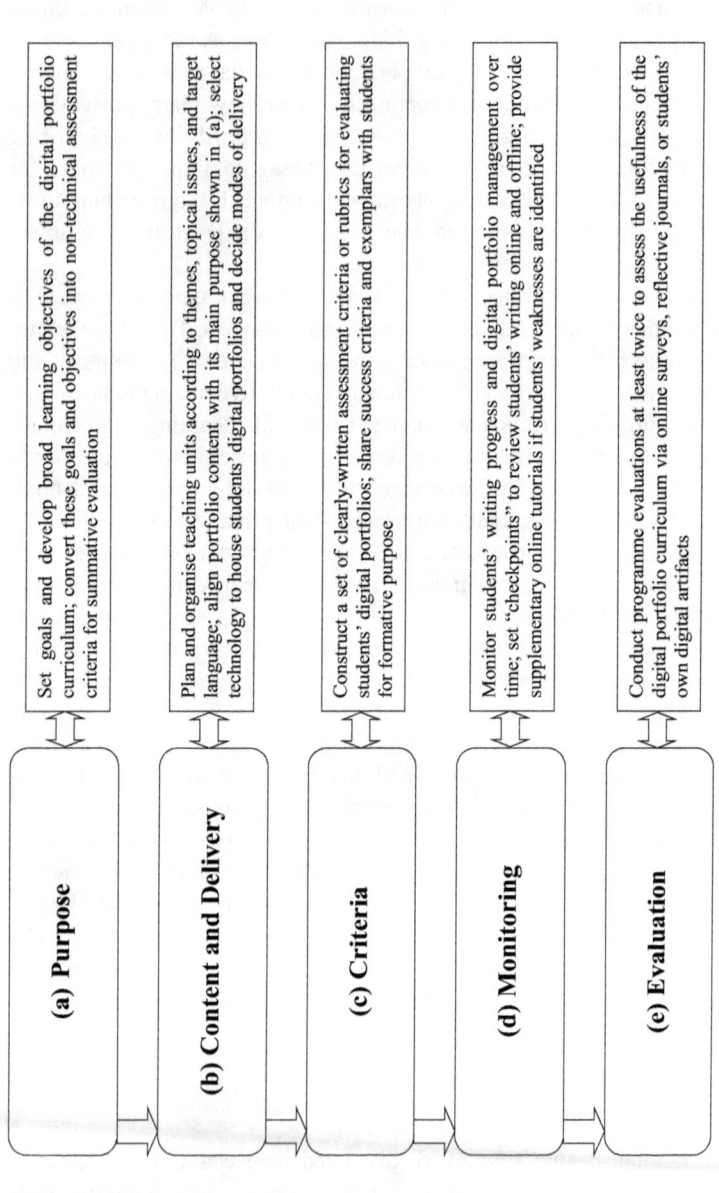

Figure 3.1 Design Framework of Digital Portfolio Curriculum
Source: adapted from Lam, 2018a, p. 35.

procedure by comparing and contrasting its various components with Delett et al.'s (2001) and Moya and O'Malley's (1994) portfolio assessment frameworks for English as a second/foreign language students in the U.S. The validation procedure involved applications of the framework components to six qualitative case studies that the first author investigated for a medium-scale, public-funded research project awarded in 2015. Parts of the project data and curriculum framework were audited by two well-renowned assessment scholars externally. The design framework has five components: (a) purpose, (b) content and delivery, (c) criteria, (d) monitoring, and (e) evaluation (Lam, 2018a, p. 35). Although this curriculum framework was originally created for print writing portfolios, it can also be applicable to digital portfolio programmes since both print and digital portfolios place great emphasis on curriculum development and renewal. However, only the latter underscores the technological dimensions of the compilation, curation, and reflection processes.

Now, we explain each component of the curriculum framework within a context of digital portfolios of writing. For (a) purpose, teachers need to have their goals and learning objectives in mind before setting up a school-based or classroom-based digital portfolio programme. The goals and objectives of the programme should be in parallel with a school's year plan. These learning objectives could also be converted into easy-to-read assessment criteria for summative evaluation. For instance, if the school plans to enhance students' literacy skills and pass rates in international language proficiency tests, teachers may consider initiating a reading-and-writing digital portfolio programme highlighting onscreen reading (e.g. flipped learning), web-based composing tasks (e.g. Wiki), and self-assessment by applying A.I.-powered editing software (e.g. Grammarly and Wordtune). Prior to implementation, the purpose of the digital portfolio programme should be succinctly drafted with colleagues and then disseminated to students, parents, and other stakeholders for endorsement. If the purpose of the digital portfolio programme is chiefly formative, the pedagogical approach could be made more individualised, creative, and multimodal without sacrificing its learning-oriented function.

Concerning (b) content and delivery, the content of digital portfolios should be planned in accordance with the existing scheme of work. Individual teaching units in the portfolio programme can be organised by broad themes (e.g. environmental protection), topical issues (e.g. the pandemic), grammar items (e.g. use of mixed tenses), and language sub-skills (teaching of reading and writing through literary texts or pop culture). These content areas should be thematically coherent to the main purpose of the portfolio programme. For instance, literacy skills could be taught under the theme of the global pandemic. Students would be encouraged to read different news reports about the COVID-19 pandemic situations and learn about the genre and associated vocabulary items with explicit instruction. Then, they would compose the same genre in multiple drafts and upload them on the digital portfolio platform for self- and peer editing. The mode of delivery could be flexible, for instance 70% face-to-face instruction, 15% blended instruction (flipped teaching), and 15% remote teaching by videoconferencing software (e.g. Zoom or Google Meet). Such an alternating hybrid delivery may broaden teachers' instructional repertoires as well as serve as a contingency plan in case class suspension happens due to natural disasters and public health crisis (Bartlett, 2022).

Speaking of (c) criteria, teachers need to develop a set of agreed-upon assessment criteria for evaluating students' digital portfolios. These assessment criteria could be created by teachers themselves, borrowed from the published literature, or co-constructed with students as meaningful learning events. Mastering how to construct an impartial and easy-to-apply rubric is equally indispensable among writing teachers. In professional scholarship, students' digital portfolios are graded by holistic, analytical, and primary trait scoring rubrics (Crusan, 2010). The details of these three types of assessment rubrics will be further discussed in Chapter 4. Apart from rubric and assessment criteria development, sharing success criteria and exemplars with students prior to summative assessments is considered a good formative assessment practice. It is because students can learn how to close the learning gaps with regard to these success criteria reflectively. Since digital portfolio platforms can expedite the entire feedback process (both synchronous and asynchronous modes), students are more likely to edit and revise their digital portfolio artefacts with multimedia feedback at one go (Lam, 2021).

For (d) monitoring, this curriculum sector refers to how teachers monitor students' writing growth and digital portfolio management throughout the programme, namely either in one school term or within an academic year. In practicality, teachers are advised to monitor students' learning curves over time when students participate in digital portfolio keeping, especially outside campus or during offline situations. To facilitate online and offline monitoring, teachers may consider setting regular "checkpoints" by designating a period, for example once every two weeks, to review students' writing progress. For instance, teachers check on whether students have uploaded essential learning artefacts on the portfolio platform for compilation, curation, and digital reflections. To warrant better writing development, teachers can comment on students' reflective pieces formatively and qualitatively, so that students can get timely feedback for further revisions (Lam, 2018b). If teachers identify students' weaknesses in writing during monitoring, they can also make informed decisions on whether they provide guided instruction during supplementary online tutorials to be held after school. Such a remedial action can make the monitoring mechanism even more pedagogical.

Regarding (e) evaluation, it is a crucial and culminating part of a digital portfolio programme. Teachers and principals can review whether the programme has made an impact on students' learning of writing and whether there are opportunities to extend the alternative pedagogy to the whole school or even to a larger community. Mid-term and end-of-term online surveys using an open-ended format with layman's terms could collect instant qualitative opinions about the usefulness of the programme. The programme evaluation may also be extracted from students' artefacts, including their digital reflections, verbal reports, blog entries, and so on by obtaining their consent. For example in a one-year programme, students are requested to upload two reflective pieces per semester on the digital portfolio platform to evaluate the programme effectiveness in terms of instructional pace, quality of feedback, and portfolio management experiences. By reviewing this online learning evidence, teachers can gather authentic and spontaneous feedback at their fingertips. Such invaluable feedback could also help teachers to make informed decisions when they further consolidate the portfolio programme. In the subsequent section, we will evaluate the practicality of utilising digital portfolios in product-oriented, process-oriented, and genre-based writing classrooms by three instructional principles.

Practicality of portfolio-based curriculum

The three pedagogical principles, enquiry, reflection, and integration, were conceptually derived from Eynon and Gambino's (2017) research project titled *Connect to Learning Network*. The project aimed to create a catalyst framework for wider digital portfolio applications at university campuses across the U.S. Enquiry refers to pedagogies that promote problem-solving, critical thinking, and exploratory learning skills. Reflection refers to students' development of metacognitive capacities throughout the processes of portfolio compilation and curation. Reflection is a core activity in the digital portfolio curriculum, which facilitates deep learning. Integration is about integrative learning experiences that connect students' learning holistically, including grade level, location, and discipline. Integrated learning enables students to transfer knowledge and skills from one subject area to another. A proper digital portfolio programme usually entails these three essential principles (Abrar-ul-Hassan et al., 2021).

In product-based writing classrooms, the digital portfolio curriculum appears to be difficult to take shape. A majority of product-based classrooms do not promote enquiry-based learning. The one-draft-one-reader approach is common, where students compose one single draft under each topic and hand it in to the only reader – their teachers for viewing and grading. Self- and peer assessments are not usually encouraged because of limited instructional hours, teachers' cynicism, and students' reluctance to participate in these formative assessment practices. Reflection is almost non-existent in product-based classrooms, given that students tend to take up a passive role in learning writing. Integrating students' learning across the board is equally taxing. The product-based classrooms emphasise grammar instruction, delivering each writing topic separately rather than comprehensively with other subject disciplines as featured in the English across the curriculum (EAC) approach. In EAC, English is used as the medium of instruction in other content courses, such as science and mathematics. This approach is said to enhance teacher language instruction as well as student subject knowledge learnt in the global language. In other words, the practicality of incorporating the digital portfolio curriculum into product-based classrooms seems to be low. However, teachers may consider adding at least one reflective component to the portfolio programme, especially near the end of each term to encourage students to review all their final drafts and ask them to showcase the best piece with reasons.

Process-oriented and digital-based portfolio classrooms seem to share lots of commonalities. Take for example these two approaches advocate compilation of multiple drafts and artefacts for critical reviews and then text revisions (an indication of enquiry learning). Either classroom context provides students with feedback-rich environments to nurture their writing development, namely self-, peer, and teacher feedback. Further, the digital portfolio classroom even provides multimodal feedback channels, for example written, verbal, audio, visual, or potentially A.I.-powered (e.g. Grammarly) to expedite the digital composing process. In process-oriented and digital-based curricula, teachers tend to adopt the learner-centred approach, allowing students ample opportunities to create, organise, monitor, and self-reflect upon works-in-progress (an instance of reflection). Reflection, thus, becomes a regular feature in process-oriented classrooms when students are expected to review and revise their drafts constantly. To facilitate integrated learning, the digital portfolio curriculum can be introduced by way of a mini multidisciplinary project comprising various subjects, including smart city living (geography and information technology), public health issues (biology), and overseas language immersion (English language). Taken together, the practicality of enacting a digital portfolio curriculum within a process-oriented writing classroom seems to be promising and facilitative.

In genre-based writing classrooms, teachers deliver explicit instruction in common written genres, namely narrative, descriptive, persuasive, expository, and creative writing. Although the genre-based and grammar-focused instructions are similar, the former emphasises mastery of a genre's textual features in relation to its immediate context and communicative functions. Meanwhile, the genre-based approach embraces the element of enquiry learning because students need to explore, synthesise, and create a genre to achieve a specific purpose. For instance students compose a draft research proposal to investigate a burning issue in society. It also supports integrative learning across subjects and modalities. Teachers may encourage students to compile artefacts of diverse genres under broad-based themes, topics, and issues, so that students can connect their learning coherently. These artefacts may include podcasts, newsfeed, social media posts (e.g. Instagram), or digital reflections created by students. In genre-based classrooms, reflection may not be a pedagogical highlight. Nevertheless, students could raise their linguistic awareness through deconstructing and then co-constructing a genre's schematic structures and lexico-grammatical features with peers and the teacher. Such a consciousness-raising task can promote students' reflective capacities. The practicality of merging the digital portfolio programme with genre-based classrooms is moderate to high although more attention should be paid to the reflective component in this approach. The last two sections comprise a self-evaluation task and a case study, which consolidate readers' understanding of how to design and develop digital portfolio-based curricula.

Self-evaluation task

Please read and think about the following questions based on what you have just learnt about digital portfolio-based curricula.

1. Which writing instructional approach – product-oriented, process-oriented, or genre-based – is congruent to my preferred teaching style?
2. Among these three instructional approaches, which one do I think is most feasible to be adopted in my educational context and why?
3. How does a digital portfolio curriculum differ from a literacy-focused English language curriculum? How do these discrepancies impede my digital portfolio application?
4. What are the possible barriers if I am about to incorporate the digital portfolio approach into a grammar-based English language curriculum? How am I going to overcome these barriers?
5. Which model – parallel, blended, or separated – belongs to a strong version of curriculum integration and which belongs to a weak version? Which curriculum integration model suits my teaching context most?

6   According to Lam's (2018a) five-step curriculum design framework, what can I do to monitor students' learning progress (i.e. the fourth step) on a chosen digital portfolio platform?
7   With 5 being most practical and 1 being least practical, how do I rate the overall practicality of adopting digital portfolios in the genre-based writing classroom?
8   The journey of designing and setting up a digital portfolio-based curriculum remains complicated. What personal, technical, and institutional challenges will I encounter if I plan to initiate one in my writing instruction?

Case study

Study the case study and then answer the following three questions.

Issue

Mr Brown, a native-speaking English teacher, is assigned to teach a Grade 7 [12-to-13-year-olds] class of mixed English language proficiency in a middle-range secondary school in Hong Kong. His students' English proficiency ranges from below average to slightly above average. Although the students are generally motivated to learn English, their writing abilities are still far from satisfactory as compared to other language skills, namely speaking. They are particularly weak at composing certain text structures and using idiomatic expressions. At times, their writings are hard to read because they made both grammatical and content errors concurrently. Content wise, their compositions are monotonous due to an obvious lack of input and deep thinking.

Action

Because of this, Mr Brown decided to implement a digital reading-and-writing portfolio programme alongside the existing grammar-focused curriculum. The programme aimed to improve students' literacy skills and increase their language awareness through online reading and writing. In this two-month programme, students were asked to read several common authentic genres, such as narrative, descriptive, and creative writing. The texts were uploaded to a class Google Drive in PDF format for easy access. These digital reading texts were used as instructional materials for teaching reading, writing, vocabulary, and grammar. Mr Brown debriefed students about the text, context, and language features of these common genres by way of explicit and implicit instruction. He adopted a wide range of delivery modes, including reader theatre, mini lectures, online peer assessment sessions, and collaborative writing projects. Near the end of each teaching unit (around 8–10 school days), students completed their reading and writing logs and drafted reader response entries, book reviews, or reflective journals in Word documents stored on the Google Drive for self-reflection as well as end-of-term summative assessment.

1 What are the pros and cons of Mr Brown's digital portfolio programme?
2 Which curriculum integration model did Mr Brown adopt and to what extent do you think this model worked well in his work context?
3 If you were Mr Brown, how would you evaluate the effectiveness of the digital reading-and-writing portfolio programme? Please elaborate on your evaluation method(s) with reasons.

Conclusion

In sum, Chapter 3 covered three major writing instructional approaches, that is product-oriented, process-oriented, and genre-based pedagogies as a contextual background to the development of digital portfolio curricula. Then, it discussed three curriculum integration models, namely parallel, blended, or separated models and reviewed the extent to which they could fit in the three writing instructional approaches. Next, the chapter unpacked Lam's (2018a) five-step curriculum design framework of writing portfolio assessment. Lastly, it evaluated the possibility of incorporating digital portfolio elements, such as enquiry, reflection, and integration into the three writing instructions with explanations. The chapter ended with one self-evaluation task plus one case study task to deepen readers' understanding.

References

Abrar-ul-Hassan, S., Douglas, D., & Turner, J. (2021). Revisiting second language portfolio assessment in a new age. *System*. https://doi.org/10.1016/j.system.2021.102652

Badge, R., & White, G. (2000). A process genre approach to the teaching writing. *ELT Journal, 54*(2), 153–160.

Bartlett, L. (2022). Specifying hybrid models of teachers' work during COVID-19. *Educational Researcher*. https://doi.org/10.3102/0013189X211069399

Burner, T. (2014). The potential formative benefits of portfolio assessment in second and foreign language writing contexts: A review of the literature. *Studies in Educational Evaluation, 43*, 139–149.

Crusan, D. (2010). *Assessment in the second language writing classroom*. The University of Michigan Press.

Curriculum Development Council. (2017). *English language education: Key learning area curriculum guide (primary 1 – secondary 6)*. Curriculum Development Council.

Delett, J. S., Barnhardt, S., & Kevorkian, J. A. (2001). A framework for portfolio assessment in the foreign language classroom. *Foreign Language Annals, 34*(6), 559–568.

Eynon, B., & Gambino, L. M. (2017). *High-impact ePortfolio practice: A catalyst for student, faculty, and institutional learning*. Stylus Publishing.

Gan, Z., & Leung, C. (2020). Illustrating formative assessment in task-based language teaching. *ELT Journal, 74*(1), 10–19.

Hyland, K. (2016). *Teaching and researching writing* (3rd ed.). Routledge.

Lam, R. (2015). Understanding EFL students' development of self-regulated learning in a process-oriented writing course. *TESOL Journal, 6*(3), 527–553.

Lam, R. (2017). Taking stock of portfolio assessment scholarship: From research to practice. *Assessing Writing, 31*, 84–97.

Lam, R. (2018a). *Portfolio assessment for the teaching and learning of writing*. Springer.

Lam, R. (2018b). Promoting self-reflection in writing: A showcase portfolio approach. In A. Burns & J. Siegel (Eds.), *International perspectives on teaching skills in ELT* (pp. 219–231). Palgrave Macmillan.

Lam, R. (2019). *Using portfolios in language teaching*. New Portfolio Series 4. SEAMEO Regional Language Centre.

Lam, R. (2021). Using ePortfolios to promote assessment of, for, as learning in EFL writing. *The European Journal of Applied Linguistics and TEFL, 10*(1), 101–120.

Lee, I. (2017). *Classroom writing assessment and feedback in L2 school contexts*. Springer.

Lee, I. (2021). Teaching writing in Hong Kong: Where are we? *Composition Studies, 49*(3), 155–159.

Lee, I., & Coniam, D. (2013). Introducing assessment for learning for EFL writing in an assessment of learning examination-driven system in Hong Kong. *Journal of Second Language Writing, 22*(1), 34–50.

Lee, I., Mak, P., & Burns, A. (2016). EFL teachers' attempts at feedback innovation in the writing classroom. *Language Teaching Research, 20*(2), 248–269.

Li, L. (2017). *New technologies and language learning*. Palgrave.

Light, T. P., Chen, H. L., & Ittelson, J. C. (2012). *Documenting learning with ePortfolios: A guide for college instructors*. Jossey-Bass.

Moya, S. S., & O'Malley, J. M. (1994). A portfolio assessment model for ESL. *The Journal of Educational Issues of Language Minority Students, 13*, 13–36.

4 Digital Portfolios for Assessment

Portfolio pedagogy versus portfolio assessment

A majority of print or digital portfolio-based scholarship focus on how teachers have applied portfolios as an alternative instructional approach in L1 and L2 classroom settings. Comparatively, little has been done to find out how teachers use digital portfolios to evaluate students' writing, namely linguistic accuracy, phrasal complexity, as well as text coherence (Lam, 2022). When portfolios are used as a pedagogical approach, teachers emphasise their fundamental features, namely collection, selection, reflection, and publication. These features help support students' learning of writing in the areas of perceptions (positive learning attitudes), motivation (improved self-efficacy beliefs), writing performance (enhanced test results), and metacognition (uptake of self-regulated thinking and composing skills; Barrot, 2021). Further, the portfolio-based instructional approach dovetails well with the process-oriented writing approach because both emphasise the iterative composing process (e.g. a writer's learning experience) rather than the writing outcomes (e.g. a writer's final summative result).

When digital portfolios are utilised for the purpose of writing assessment, the practice is called *digital portfolio assessment*. In research, the type of portfolios used for this evaluative function is assessment portfolios. Assessment portfolios are a tool to help students take stock of their learning reflectively and provide a wider spectrum of what composing skills they have learnt for grading (Lam, 2019). When portfolios are used to fulfil the evaluative role, researchers have identified four advantages. Digital portfolios could be a fair assessment tool to capture students' writing development over time as opposed to one-shot impromptu writing assessments (Yancey, 2009). They can evaluate some high-order thinking skills, such as creativity, metacognition, and critical thinking. Owing to the unique nature of deferral in grading, students have more time and space to compile evidence of

DOI: 10.4324/9781003295860-5

learning to justify their writing performance (Curtis, 2018). Since students are mostly digitally competent these days, they are likely to have intrinsic motivation to develop their digital portfolios for assessment (Keen, 2021).

Despite these merits, scholars have pointed out six barriers. First, for teachers, workload is an issue because other than students' final drafts, teachers need to read and give comments on students' interim drafts plus other multimodal artefacts. The marking load is likely to double as compared to marking students' single-draft compositions. Second, teachers' knowledge and skills in grading digital portfolios proficiently would be a cause for concern, since a portfolio usually comprises more than one genre, one modality, and one artefact, not to mention the skills in scoring students' reflective pieces (Yancey, 2015). Third, generating timely and appropriate feedback on digital portfolio tools can be a challenge. Teachers need to be assessment literate to provide quality formative and summative written feedback to students (Lee, 2019). Fourth, for students, managing a number of multimodal artefacts for grading in a semester is taxing, especially for those who are less academically able (Lam, 2013). Fifth, students may simply focus on mastering technological skills over composing skills when they construct their digital portfolios. They may, incorrectly assume that, designing a flashy portfolio interface is likely to get higher marks (Renwick, 2017). Sixth, when students realise that their portfolios are assessed, they may not be willing to engage in authentic reflective practices. Instead, they may perform to the task requirements (McGarr & O'Gallchóir, 2020). The following section describes how teachers can adopt digital portfolios to evaluate students' writing.

Digital portfolios for writing evaluation

This section starts with an introduction of the four purposes of writing assessment, followed by a discussion on how digital portfolios are adopted in classroom-based and standardised assessment. Practical strategies regarding how to evaluate students' writing formatively and summatively are then suggested. Writing assessment typically serves formative, summative, diagnostic, and evaluative purposes. The first two are associated with the classroom instruction context, whereas the other two are related to the programme management. The formative purpose of assessment denotes how teachers assist students to develop and improve writing with constructive written feedback (qualitative commentaries), positive reinforcement (rewards on good works), and encouragement (emotional support; Lee, 2017). It intends to help students to learn the skill of writing. The summative purpose of assessment is to sum up and grade students' writing near the end of a teaching unit or a semester. It aims to summarise students' learning of writing at regular intervals. The diagnostic purpose of assessment refers to any pre-assessments, which differentiate students' diverse learning needs to inform curriculum planning and to consolidate writing instruction with students' assessment data (e.g. placement test results). It operates at the programme level. The evaluative purpose of assessment is to make students' learning accountable to key stakeholders, namely school sponsoring bodies and the ministry of education personnel through systematic programme evaluations. It serves to support quality assurance, external audit, and benchmarking exercises.

The following two paragraphs depict the differences between classroom-based digital portfolio assessment (CBPA), for example school-based digital portfolio programmes and large-scale, standardised digital portfolio assessment (SDPA), that is European Language Portfolio in Europe or LinguaFolio in the U.S. in terms of purpose, syllabus, applications, scoring methods, role of learners and teachers, and impact. This discussion serves to unpack the rationale behind these two portfolio assessments as they fulfil different functions. The purpose of CBPA is chiefly formative and occasionally summative for internal reporting, whereas the purpose of SDPA is summative and evaluative. At times, teachers may use the assessment information to fine-tune their instructional approaches in the next academic year. The syllabus of CBPA tends to be negotiable, context-specific, and descriptive, while the syllabus of SDPA is relatively restrictive and prescriptive to achieve fairness. The application of CBPA is varied and flexible, emphasising the use of authentic assessment tools (e.g. school portals, common digital portfolio platforms, or learning management systems), but the application of SDPA is standardised by respective exam boards, limiting learner's choice in the portfolio development process.

The scoring methods of CBPA involve multiple parties, namely students, peers, teachers, peers, and the community, for example social media users, whereas SDPA is mostly scored by qualified raters and/or assessment experts. In CBPA, students take up the role of active learners and knowledge co-constructors with their classmates and teachers, and teachers assume the role of writing coaches to facilitate students' learning of writing in a less threatening virtual environment. Yet, in SDPA, students are considered passive test-takers and teachers have no direct involvement in the digital portfolio scoring process. Because CBPA is formative and low-stakes, it may create a positive impact on students' learning. In contrast, SDPA tends to a create negative impact on students' learning, as it is usually high-stakes and determines students' future study pathways. For easy reference, a summary of the disparities between classroom-based and standardised digital portfolio assessment is illustrated in Table 4.1.

Table 4.1 Classroom-Based Versus Standardised Digital Portfolio Assessment

	Classroom-Based Digital Portfolio Assessment (CBPA)	Standardised Digital Portfolio Assessment (SDPA)
Purpose	Mostly formative but occasionally summative for internal reporting	Summative and evaluative
Syllabus	Negotiable among learners and teachers; descriptive; and context-specific; prepared by teachers	Usually restrictive and prescriptive; prepared by exam authority personnel
Applications	Varied, authentic, and flexible such as school portals, common digital portfolio tools (Seesaw), and learning management systems	Standardised portal designed by exam authority
Scoring Methods	Involve multiple assessors, such as students, teachers, parents, and the community	Scored by external raters only
Role of Student	Active learners; portfolio designers; knowledge co-constructors	Passive test-takers; portfolio content suppliers
Role of Teacher	Writing coaches and learning facilitators	Outsiders not having direct involvement in assessment process
Impact	Creates moderate-to-positive impact on student learning	Likely to create negative impact on student learning owing to high-stakes nature

To evaluate students' writing formatively in digital portfolios, teachers may consider the following strategies. (1) Teachers provide students' artefacts with formative feedback, for example rubric-referenced statements, written commentary highlighting areas of improvement, oral feedback recorded in audio files, and synchronous responses on weblog posts. (2) Teachers provide recommendations on how to facilitate students' digital portfolio compilation process, namely giving personalised advice on the selection of digital portfolio platform and creation of hyperlinks and offering tips on how to organise multimodal portfolio artefacts by type, genre, date, and rationale. (3) Teachers follow the principle of deferral of grading by not assigning summative grades on students' artefacts until revision is satisfactorily made because grades imply that learning is completed. (4) Teachers help students perform self-reflection by commenting on their reflective pieces. Such e-feedback could be presented in the form of speech bubbles and annotated texts to create a supportive environment for co-regulation of learning (Allal, 2020). (5) Teachers organise student–parent–teacher virtual conferences to communicate with one another as to how to achieve the learning outcomes with regard to students' set goals and their current writing performance. These tripartite talks are likely to develop a better understanding of how to fulfil the assessment expectations of digital portfolios. (6) Teachers can empower students' learning of writing through promoting self-regulated learning, which includes iterative processes of goal-setting, monitoring, adjusting, and revising in the digital portfolio journey (Andrade & Brookhart, 2016). As claimed by Lee (2016), putting students at the centre of learning enables sustained writing development, learner independence, and uptake of metacognitive skills.

To evaluate students' writing summatively, teachers may consider these tactics. (1) Teachers assign a letter grade (A being excellent and D being marginal pass) or a numerical score (100 being full marks and 40 being a pass mark) to students' digital portfolios relating to the assessment criteria, which has been made available and clear to students before grading. (2) Teachers require students to rationalise the representative works they selected for summative grading. By doing so, teachers can assess students' final portfolio artefacts more accurately. (3) Teachers propose a fair assessment weighting when they construct scoring rubrics. Lam (2020) has suggested that the scoring rubric of a digital portfolio include a balanced ratio of the process grade (30%; e.g. effort shown in revision and portfolio management), the product grade (50%; e.g. assessment of the completed digital portfolio against the task requirements/ scoring rubric), and the reflective grade (20%; e.g. evidence of reflection and growth). (4) If the digital portfolio programme is merely part of the English language curriculum, teachers may adopt a pass or fail grade plus identify the strengths and weaknesses of students' composing, thinking, and technological skills as justifications. (5) Teachers and principals may consider utilising the grades or scores of students' digital portfolios to achieve diverse external accountability purposes, such as reporting students' writing performances and language abilities in university admission exercises, school-based assessments (as parts of the public exams, e.g. in the U.K. General Certificate of Secondary Education (GCSE)), and placement tests for class-level or grade-level allocation (Lam, 2019). The subsequent section discusses the relationship between digital portfolios and assessment of/for/as learning respectively.

Digital portfolios and assessment of/for/as learning

In the past two decades, three major assessment paradigms have emerged, including assessment *of* learning (hereafter AOL), assessment *for* learning (hereafter AFL), and assessment *as* learning (hereafter AAL). AOL refers to summative assessment, which serves to grade students' learning, whereas AFL equates to formative assessment, which intends to improve students' learning. AAL is part of assessment for learning, yet the former emphasises students' self-reflective practices. An example of AOL is the large-scale, standardised test/exam in various educational jurisdictions, such as IELTS and GCSE. At times, scholars considered high-stakes internal school exams as AOL. One common indication of AFL is effective instructional practices, which emphasises high-frequency and high-quality teacher–student interactions, that is learner-centric pedagogies with a focus on moments of contingency (Bennett, 2011). An instance of AAL is students' metacognitive development through active participation in various self-assessment tasks to close the learning gaps (Dann, 2014; Earl, 2013). Although the three assessment paradigms serve multiple purposes, they tend to be in tension when applied simultaneously (Lau, 2016). A case in point is that AOL is usually predominant amid the implementation of AFL/AAL-oriented practices, such as process writing, focused written feedback, and rubric-referenced self-assessment, because students remain more concerned about their exam results than mastery of composing skills (Lam, 2018; Zhang & Hyland, 2018).

Utilising digital portfolios to achieve AOL appears to provide an alternative approach to writing assessment, particularly when digital portfolios are considered one form of authentic assessment (Lam, 2021). However, standardised digital portfolio assessment may create the issues of content validity, scoring consistency, confidentiality, and the digital divide. First, unless there are clear-cut assessment rubrics describing how to score various aspects of a digital portfolio, it is challenging for raters to grade students' composing and technological skills separately and accurately, since certain fancy portfolio interfaces may distract raters' evaluative judgements (Lam, 2020). Second, external raters may find it taxing to score multi-genre and multimodal digital portfolios consistently because they are likely to experience grading fatigue by viewing and judging a wide array of hyperlinks, intertextual artefacts, and digital attachments for a prolonged period, not to mention the fact that these artefacts are hard to compare. Third, as students' digital portfolios are made accessible online, their privacy could be easily disclosed to the public, such as reflection on weaknesses in writings or a confession of failure in learning. The acts of digital reflection would make students fall prey to doxxing and cyberbullying (Wilson et al., 2018). Fourth, the phenomenon of digital divide may diminish test fairness and positive washback of standardised digital portfolio assessment because not every student has equal access to electronic gadgets and computer infrastructure (tablets, laptops, and stable Wi-Fi connection) in their schools and/or families (Hockly & Dudeney, 2018).

To support students' learning, AFL fits in with classroom-based digital portfolios. It embodies several learning-oriented characteristics that can be found in digital portfolios, such as self- and peer assessment, collaborative writing, sharing of success criteria and exemplars, and flipped learning (Payant & Zuniga, 2022; Zhang & Chen, 2022). AFL underscores the importance of iterative feedback processes, which support students' compilation of their digital artefacts (to be discussed in Chapter 5). It is because teachers can provide students with synchronous online feedback to improve learning through revision of works-in-progress and instruction through additional online tutorials for consolidation. To help special educational needs or less-proficient students, teachers may opt for recording parts of their corrective written feedback and mini-lectures in audio files and uploading them on designated digital portfolio platforms, such as Wix, Schoology, or Padlet for course review (Lam, 2019). Those instant formative assessment data, for example teachers' verbal feedback and online responses to students' enquiries, could serve to fine-tune teachers' remote or in-person teaching in a reflective manner (Farrell & Stanclik, 2021). Since AFL-driven digital portfolio assessment involves collaboration among students, peers, teachers, parents, and virtual audiences, it is likely to promote a community of practice that facilitates co-construction of new meanings in students' hypertexts and showcases interactive use of multimodal source materials, namely audio, video, pictorial, virtual reality-generated formats to create new discourse (Yancey, 2019).

Like AFL, AAL improves students' learning of writing. In the assessment literature, AAL is part of AFL, but it is considered a learner-centred rather than a teacher-assisted version of AFL (Xiang et al., 2021). AAL has one significant digital portfolio assessment feature that is students' self-reflective practices (Earl, 2013). These reflective components entail a tripartite procedure, namely goal-setting, monitoring, and revising, which simulates Zimmerman's self-regulated learning cyclical model applied in general education (Clark, 2012). When AAL is prioritised in digital portfolio assessment, it promotes effective writing instruction, which aligns with good practices in writing assessment. Graham and Alves (2021, pp. 1616–1617) listed out 12 evidence-based formative instructional practices. Of these, four practices are relatable to AAL-oriented activities, namely (1) setting goals for writing; (2) teaching general and genre-specific strategies for planning, revising, editing, and regulating the writing process; (3) giving feedback to students about their standards of writing and their writing progress for closing the learning gaps; and (4) mobilising digital tools that make composing easier. These formative practices denote that learning and assessing writing can be positively integrated. As claimed by

Dann (2014) and Ryan (2014), assessment is fundamentally part of learning, because learning how to self-assess one's writing, an instance of AAL, is an indispensable twenty-first-century skill that enhances students' metacognitive capacities and promotes knowledge transfer across subject disciplines and grade levels (or beyond students' graduation).

As mentioned earlier, AOL is likely to dominate when juxtaposed with AFL and AAL in digital portfolio assessment. Teachers may consider synergising the three assessment paradigms in a strategic way. For example AAL learning activities can be placed at the core of concentric circles. These tasks encourage self-reflective and collaborative writing practices, so that students learn how to set goals, monitor the goals, and revise their writings accordingly (Lee, 2016). AFL instructional approaches are put in the second outer layer of the concentric circles. They refer to learner-centred pedagogies that support uptake of multisource and multimodal feedback to help students close the learning gaps if discrepancies between their set goals and assessment expectations arise (Dann, 2018). Afterward, AOL, equivalent to an exam-oriented learning context, is positioned on the periphery, the outermost layer of the concentric circles. These high-stakes exam syllabus can convert into meaningful instructional materials for AFL-focused lesson design and AAL-oriented learning tasks (Yeo, 2021). Combining AFL, AAL, and AOL in digital portfolio assessment appears to be efficient, practical as well as manageable for busy teachers (Jones & Saville, 2016). The AFL–AAL–AOL synergy is displayed in Figure 4.1.

According to Lam (2021), there are three common classroom strategies that align AFL, AAL, and AOL for digital portfolios. These strategies are applicable to both in-person and remote instruction, depending on the teaching and learning environment. First, teachers introduce dynamic pre-assessment preparation as a consciousness-raising strategy. Students are asked to identify a frequently tested genre in school-based or public assessment past papers from the last five years or to self-evaluate the strengths and weaknesses of an exemplar against the mark scheme published by an official assessment organisation. They are advised to use the highlighting and annotative note functions of a PDF reader when completing the tasks. Second, teachers task students with creating student-generated mock assessment papers as a deep learning approach. Students rarely have opportunities to construct assessment items so the process can raise their awareness of the key features of an assessment paper. When performing this collaborative writing task, students can use Google Forms or Google Docs as a tool. In case where classes are conducted remotely through online modes, to facilitate virtual discussion, students may choose one videoconferencing software tool like Zoom. Third, teachers may try out post-assessment follow-up as a consolidation strategy. They can use the students' assessment results as input to fine-tune their in-person or remote instruction, such as re-teaching

Digital Portfolios for Assessment 45

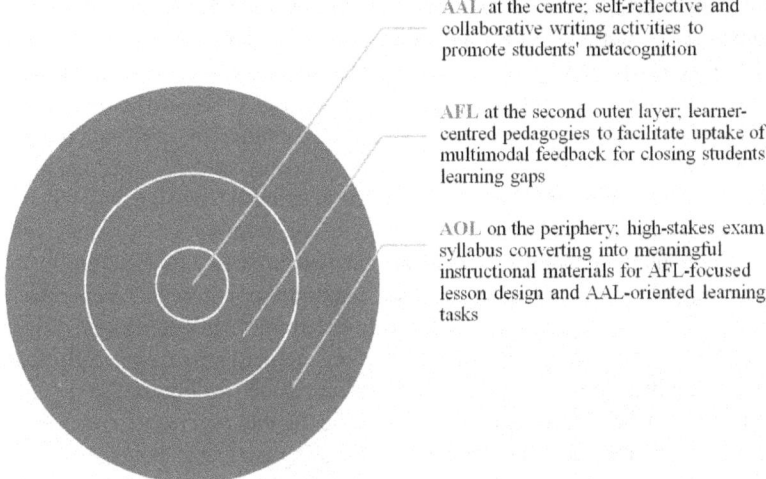

AAL at the centre; self-reflective and collaborative writing activities to promote students' metacognition

AFL at the second outer layer; learner-centred pedagogies to facilitate uptake of multimodal feedback for closing students' learning gaps

AOL on the periphery; high-stakes exam syllabus converting into meaningful instructional materials for AFL-focused lesson design and AAL-oriented learning tasks

Figure 4.1 AFL–AAL–AOL Synergy

a problematic grammatical structure. Furthermore, teachers can invite students to rewrite the same composition by having them identify which aspects they have done well and which aspects they need improvement at the second attempt. Students can complete these self-reflective activities on a digital portfolio platform for easy onscreen reading, cross-referencing, and peer commenting like Schoology, which facilitates synchronous exchange of textual and audio peer feedback. The next section outlines three types of scoring rubrics and their construction procedures.

Procedures of rubric construction

In writing assessment, there are three evaluation methods, including holistic scoring, primary trait scoring, and analytic scoring (Hamp-Lyons & Condon, 2000). Holistic scoring, aka impression marking, is mostly adopted in standardised writing assessments, in which a large number of compositions are read and scored in a norm-referenced fashion. Primary trait scoring, emphasising an evaluation of one key aspect of writing, is generally criterion-referenced and applied in individual classroom settings to serve the purpose of diagnosis and summative evaluation. Analytic scoring is also referred to as multiple traits scoring (Hamp-Lyons, 1995), because it highlights a comprehensive evaluation of a piece of writing in terms of its major elements. The theoretical basis of holistic scoring is that writing ability is considered a complete entity and scoring a text holistically is more significant than scoring its parts, whereas the rationale for primary trait scoring is that different written genres may demand the writer to consider the purpose, context, and audience when they are composing (Lam, 2018). The theoretical underpinning of analytical scoring lies in the fact that writing is learnt as a comprehensive skill not a series of isolated components. Regardless of their similar rationale, one major difference between holistic and analytic scoring is that the former evaluates students' writing in an aggregate manner and the latter evaluates students' writing in each key aspect, namely content, organisation, style, and grammar comprehensively.

The benefits of holistic scoring are time-saving and cost-effective as the scoring procedure can accommodate a substantial number of papers at a time. However, its major drawback is to reach inter-rater agreement, which diminishes the authenticity of text reading. Regarding primary trait scoring, the advantage is an in-depth evaluation of one specific trait of a genre, whereas teachers need expertise in constructing and applying the rubrics in context. The pros and cons of analytical scoring are that it can evaluate students' all-round writing ability accurately, but the scoring procedure could be time-consuming. Teachers may also find it perplexed to interpret various sub-categories in the rubrics when they score a digital portfolio analytically (Wolcott, 1998). Taken together, if teachers score students' digital portfolios to achieve the learning-oriented purpose, they may consider adopting analytical and primary trait scoring methods. However, it takes additional time and effort to construct the rubrics and participate in the scoring process. If teachers score students' digital portfolios as an end-of-term summative evaluation, they may choose holistic scoring. It is because this method is relatively straightforward and efficient although training in reading papers holistically and compiling anchor papers of various writing abilities are equally taxing (Tomas et al., 2019). With that said, teachers may combine holistic and analytic scoring methods when they grade students' digital portfolios to fulfil formative and summative purposes of assessment simultaneously (Lam, 2022).

To facilitate the aforementioned scoring methods, the rubric construction procedures are described here. A rubric is defined as a detailed scoring guide, which assists summative grading of students' digital portfolio assignments. It has three major elements, such as (1) criteria, (2) descriptors, and (3) levels of performance (Lam, 2019). For instance criteria refer to iterative processes of digital portfolio development, that is collection, curation, reflection, and dissemination as well as students' digital competence when compiling the artefacts. Descriptors depict how those criteria are achieved by students over time. They appear in the form of qualitative performance indicators. Levels of performance equate to a rating scale, which classifies students' diverse abilities to compile and manage their digital portfolios, be they numerical (30 – seriously deficient to 100 – extremely outstanding), alphabetical (Grades A, B to D), or domain-specific ranks (showing creativity in digital artefacts/ability to monitor writing development/mastery of proficient artefact curation).

In holistic scoring, there are normally two columns in the rubrics, with the first displaying the levels of performance (e.g. marks: 100–0 and/or labels: exemplary to unacceptable) and the second showing the descriptors linked with respective levels of performance (see Table 4.2). Unlike the holistic scoring rubrics, primary trait rubrics contain a writing prompt of the task, the primary trait to be evaluated and five to seven levels of performance with detailed descriptors at each level (e.g. 0–4; for details, see Table 4.3). Analytical scoring rubrics have three columns. Criteria are put

Table 4.2 Holistic Scoring Guide for Digital Portfolio

Level and Score	Description
Exemplary 100–90	The portfolio **evidently** shows the processes of collection, selection, reflection, and dissemination. It demonstrates the author's growth and achievements through a **wide** range of multimodal artefacts. Its design and interface reflect the author's creativity, communicative competence, digital literacy, and collaborative skills **to a very large extent**. The writings are error-free and highly reader-friendly.
Very Good 89.9–70	The portfolio **adequately** shows the processes of collection, selection, reflection, and dissemination. It demonstrates the author's growth and achievements through an **average** range of multimodal artefacts. Its design and interface reflect the author's creativity, communicative competence, digital literacy, and collaborative skills **to a certain extent**. The writings are mostly accurate with some minor grammatical errors.
Average 69.9–40	The portfolio **partially** shows the processes of collection, selection, reflection, and dissemination, especially for reflection. It demonstrates the author's growth and achievements through a **limited** range of multimodal artefacts. Its design and interface reflect the author's creativity, communicative competence, digital literacy, and collaborative skills **to a lesser extent**. At times, the writings are **hard** to follow owing to improper use of vocabulary and text incoherence.

(*Continued*)

48 Digital Portfolios for Assessment

Table 4.2 (Continued)

Level and Score	Description
Below average 39.9–20	The portfolio clearly **lacks** the processes of collection, selection, reflection, and dissemination. It is **unable** to demonstrate the author's growth and achievements with valid learning evidence. Its design and interface **cannot** reflect the author's creativity, communicative competence, digital literacy, and collaborative skills. The writings have frequent semantic, rhetorical, and/or grammatical errors, which impede comprehension. The author needs to rework on the portfolio.
Score: /100	Other comments: Signed by teacher:

Table 4.3 Primary Trait Rubrics for Digital Portfolio

Legend	**Primary Trait**: Substantiation of students' reflection by way of curating pertinent multimodal artefacts, such as text-based, audio, video, hyper-textual, or graphic ones. **Scoring Rationale**: This portfolio task is to promote students' active reflection upon their digital composing skills by validating the evidence of learning compiled on various digital portfolio sites.

Level and Score	Description
Level 5 25–20 marks	*Topmost substantiation.* The author engages in a deep level of reflection by analyzing multimodal artefacts critically and comprehensively. She is able to cite robust evidence to support the reflective statements. The digital reflection is creative, evaluative, and compelling to promote the author's learning of writing effectively.
Level 4 19.9–15 marks	*Maximum substantiation.* The author engages in an insightful reflection by curating multimodal artefacts systematically. She can cite multiple sources of learning evidence to support the reflective statements. The digital reflection is well-written and constructive to promote the author's learning of writing positively.
Level 3 14.9–10 marks	*Adequate substantiation.* The author engages in an ordinary reflection by showcasing multimodal artefacts haphazardly. She manages to cite related learning evidence to support the reflective statements albeit not very proficiently. The digital reflection is anecdotal and descriptive, which may not help enhance the author's learning of writing sufficiently.
Level 2 9.9–5 marks	*Minimum substantiation.* The author shows sporadic attempts at reflecting upon multimodal artefacts in her portfolio. She apparently encounters difficulties in citing proper learning evidence to support the reflective statements. The digital reflection is somewhat sketchy, which is not likely to contribute to the author's growth in writing development.
Level 0 Below 5 marks	*Lack of substantiation.* The author shows no attempts at reflecting upon any multimodal artefacts for further evaluation. She is unable to cite multiple sources of learning evidence to support the reflective statements. The digital reflection is almost non-existent, given that the author is not aware of this essential component.

Table 4.4 Analytical Scoring Guide for Digital Portfolio

Levels of Performance/Criteria	Exemplary	Accomplished	Developing	Beginning	Score
Collection	Skilful in creating and compiling most appropriate artefacts in the portfolio (10–9)	Able to create and compile appropriate artefacts in the portfolio (8–6)	Marginally able to create and compile relevant artefacts in the portfolio (5–3)	Obviously unable to create and compile right artefacts in the portfolio (2–0)	= /10
Curation	Skilful in organising a broad range of artefacts to facilitate effective learning of writing (10–9)	Able to organise a wide range of artefacts to facilitate effective learning of writing (8–6)	Minimally able to organise related artefacts to facilitate learning of writing (5–3)	Unable to organise proper artefacts to support learning of writing (2–0)	= /10
Reflection	Skilful in reflecting upon most appropriate evidence to showcase one's best ability (10–9)	Able to reflect upon appropriate evidence to showcase one's best ability (8–6)	Barely able to reflect upon suitable evidence, but haphazardly choose completed works to represent one's writing development (5–3)	Incapable of neither performing reflection nor selecting appropriate artefacts to showcase one's best ability (2–0)	= /10
Digital Competence	Showing exemplary skills in operating various functions of the digital portfolio tool to improve writing (10–9)	Showing substantial skills in operating various functions of the digital portfolio tool to improve writing (8–6)	Showing adequate skills in operating various functions of the digital portfolio tool to improve writing (5–3)	Showing insufficient skills in operating various functions of the digital portfolio tool to improve writing (2–0)	= /10
					Score: / 40

Note: The digital portfolio carries 40% of the course grade.

Source: adapted from Lam, 2019.

in the first column (the y axis), namely collection, curation, reflection, and so on. Levels of performance in terms of qualitative labels are located in the first row (the top x axis), namely novice, apprentice, proficient, and distinguished. The sub-scores of each criterion are placed in the third column (the y axis). The middle grids comprise descriptors, which explain the criteria and levels of performance in detail (see Table 4.4). The penultimate section presents a mini-research task, which encourages readers to investigate teachers' perceptions of the AFL–AAL–AOL synergy through digital portfolios and their views on the effectiveness of three portfolio scoring rubrics when used to improve students' writing.

Mini-research task

Study the following instructions and conduct a mini-research study through your personal connection or in your teaching practicum school.

Part A

In the school context, synergising the learning and grading purposes of digital portfolio assessment appears to be under-represented when compared to other aspects of portfolio assessment research. Hence, conduct an online questionnaire with no more than eight 5-point Likert-scale items to examine teachers' perceptions of AFL–AAL–AOL synergy on various digital portfolio platforms. You may include the following pointers in your questionnaire:

(1) Pre-assessment preparation as a consciousness-raising strategy (e.g. deepening students' understanding of assessment syllabus)
(2) Student-generated mock test paper as a deep learning approach (e.g. developing students' metacognitive skills)
(3) Provision of synchronous e-feedback throughout digital portfolio compilation as a learning support mechanism (e.g. e-feedback for text revision)
(4) Post-assessment follow-up as a consolidation pedagogical strategy (e.g. re-teaching of weakest grammar structures)
(5) Others

After collecting the questionnaire data, analyse them using descriptive statistics and identify how teachers perceived the usefulness of different instructional strategies that positively aligned the learning and grading purposes of digital portfolio assessment.

Part B

Conduct a focus-group interview with three in-service teachers of different seniority. Encourage them to discuss (1) how they generally perceive the holistic, primary trait, and analytical scoring rubrics in terms of their advantages and drawbacks, (2) which scoring rubrics are learning-oriented and practical to be adopted in writing classrooms, and (3) how these rubrics may assist students to improve their self-assessment and revision skills within the context of digital portfolio assessment. After transcribing and coding the data, identify key themes that generate new understanding of how to apply the three scoring rubrics to evaluate digital portfolios formatively and summatively.

Conclusion

Chapter 4 spelt out major differences between digital portfolio pedagogy and digital portfolio assessment. Next, the chapter explained the four purposes of writing assessment and the distinctions between classroom-based digital portfolio programmes and standardised digital portfolio assessments. Further, it illustrated practical strategies on how to assess students' writing effectively with digital portfolios. Then, the chapter discussed how teachers can use digital portfolios to achieve assessment of/for/as learning in the writing classrooms. Afterwards, it introduced three oft-cited scoring methods and their respective rubric construction procedures for easy reference. The chapter closed with a mini-research task, which enhanced readers' conceptual understanding of salient issues in digital portfolio assessment.

References

Allal, L. (2020). Assessment and the co-regulation of learning in the classroom. *Assessment in Education: Principles, Policy & Practice, 27*(4), 332–349.

Andrade, H., & Brookhart, S. M. (2016). The role of classroom assessment in supporting self-regulated learning. In D. Laveault & L. Allal (Eds.), *Assessment for learning: Meeting the challenge of implementation: The enabling power of assessment* (pp. 293–309). Springer.

Barrot, J. S. (2021). Effects of Facebook-based e-portfolio on ESL learners' writing performance. *Language, Culture and Curriculum, 34*(1), 95–111.

Bennett, R. E. (2011). Formative assessment: A critical review. *Assessment in Education: Principles, Policy & Practice, 18*(1), 5–25.

Clark, I. (2012). Formative assessment: Assessment is for self-regulated learning. *Educational Psychology Review, 24*(2), 205–249.

Curtis, A. (2018). Portfolios. In J. I. Liontas (Ed.), *The TESOL encyclopedia of English language teaching* (1st ed.). https://doi.org/10.1002/9781118784235.eelt0326

Dann, R. (2014). Assessment *as* learning: Blurring the boundaries of assessment and learning for theory, policy and practice. *Assessment in Education: Principles, Policy & Practice, 21*(2), 149–166.

Dann, R. (2018). *Developing feedback for pupil learning*. Routledge.

Earl, L. M. (2013). *Assessment as learning: Using classroom assessment to maximize student learning* (2nd ed.). Corwin.

Farrell, T. S. C., & Stanclik, C. (2021). "COVID-19 is an opportunity to rediscover ourselves": Reflections of a novice EFL teacher in Central America. *RELC Journal*. https://doi.org/10.1177/0033688220981778

Graham, S., & Alves, R. A. (2021). Research and teaching writing. *Reading and Writing, 34*, 1613–1621.

Hamp-Lyons, L. (1995). Uncovering possibilities for a constructivist paradigm for writing assessment (review). *College Composition and Communication, 46*, 446–455.

Hamp-Lyons, L., & Condon, W. (2000). *Assessing the portfolio: Issues for research, theory and practice*. Hampton Press.

Hockly, N., & Dudeney, G. (2018). Current and future digital trends in ELT. *RELC Journal, 49*(2), 164–178.

Jones, N., & Saville, N. (2016). *Learning oriented assessment: A systemic approach*. Cambridge University Press.

Keen, J. (2021). Teaching writing: Process, practice and policy. *Changing English*. https://doi.org/10.1080/1358684X.2021.2008229

Lam, R. (2013). Two portfolio systems: EFL students' perceptions of writing ability, text improvement, and feedback. *Assessing Writing, 18*(2), 132–153.

Lam, R. (2018). *Portfolio assessment for the teaching and learning of writing*. Springer.

Lam, R. (2019). *Using portfolios in language teaching*. New Portfolio Series 4. SEAMEO Regional Language Centre.

Lam, R. (2020). Why reinvent the wheel? E-portfolios are for learning. *ELT Journal, 74*(4), 488–491.

Lam, R. (2021). Using ePortfolios to promote assessment of, for, as learning in EFL writing. *The European Journal of Applied Linguistics and TEFL, 10*(1), 101–120.

Lam, R. (2022). Assessing creative writing formatively and summatively with e-portfolios: A case study in Hong Kong. In B. Chamcharatsri & A. Iida (Eds.), *International perspectives on using creative writing in second language education: Supporting language learners' proficiency, identity and creative expression* (pp. 171–188). Routledge.

Lau, A. M. Z. (2016). "Formative good, summative bad"? – A review of the dichotomy in assessment literature. *Journal of Further and Higher Education, 40*(4), 509–525.

Lee, I. (2016). Putting students at the centre of classroom L2 writing assessment. *The Canadian Modern Language Review, 72*(2), 258–280.

Lee, I. (2017). *Classroom writing assessment and feedback in L2 school contexts.* Springer.

Lee, I. (2019). Teachers' frequently asked questions about focused written corrective feedback. *TESOL Journal, 10*(3). https://doi.org/10.1002/tesj.427

McGarr, O., & O'Gallchóir, C. (2020). The futile quest for honesty in reflective writing: Recognising self-criticism as a form of self-enhancement. *Teaching in Higher Education, 25*(7), 902–908.

Payant, C., & Zuniga, M. (2022). Learners' flow experience during peer revision in a virtual writing course during the global pandemic. *System, 105*, 102715.

Renwick, M. (2017). *Digital portfolios in the classroom: Showcasing and assessing student work.* Association for Supervision and Curriculum Development.

Ryan, M. (2014). Reflexive writers: Re-thinking writing development and assessment in schools. *Assessing Writing, 22*, 60–74.

Tomas, C., Whitt, E., Lavelle-Hill, R., & Severn, K. (2019). Modeling holistic marks with analytic rubrics. *Frontiers in Education, 4*(89). https://doi.org/10.3389/feduc.2019.00089

Wilson, C., Slade, C., Kirby, M., Downer, T., Fisher, M., & Nuessler, S. (2018). Digital ethics and the use of ePortfolio: A scoping review of the literature. *International Journal of ePortfolio, 8*(2), 115–125.

Wolcott, W. (1998). *An overview of writing assessment: Theory, research, and practice.* National Council of Teachers of English.

Xiang, X., Yuan, R., & Yu, B. (2021). Implementing assessment as learning in the L2 writing classroom: A Chinese case. *Assessment & Evaluation in Higher Education.* https://doi.org/10.1080/02602938.2021.1965539

Yancey, K. B. (2009). Electronic portfolios a decade into the twenty-first century: What we know, what we need to know. *Peer Review, 11*(1), 28–32.

Yancey, K. B. (2015). Grading ePortfolios: Tracing two approaches, their advantages, and their disadvantages. *Theory into Practice, 54*, 301–308.

Yancey, K. B. (Ed.). (2019). *ePortfolio as curriculum: Models and practices for developing students' ePortfolio literacy.* Stylus Publishing.

Yeo, M. (2021). "Experiencing theory first-hand was delightful and informative": Bridging the theory-practice gap in online language assessment training. *Iranian Journal of Language Teaching Research, 9*(3), 93–116.

Zhang, M., & Chen, W. (2022). Assessing collaborative writing in the digital age: An exploratory study. *Journal of Second Language Writing.* https://doi.org/10.1016/j.jslw.2022.100868

Zhang, Z. V., & Hyland, K. (2018). Student engagement with teacher and automated feedback on L2 writing. *Assessing Writing, 36*, 90–102.

5 Feedback in Digital Portfolios

Feedback in portfolio assessment

Collection, selection, and reflection are essential staples of portfolio assessment. To lubricate these iterative components, feedback plays an indispensable role in activating, catalysing, and regulating students' current and prior knowledge to create new discourse in the entire composing process (see Chapter 1). Feedback is defined as useful assessment information, be it formative or summative, which informs teachers and students to improve teaching and learning respectively. Feedback can help students to "feed forward". With guidance from their teachers, they can utilise pertinent assessment data to set goals and inform their future learning. In addition, they can engage in the cognitive process of "feeding back" by reviewing and evaluating their prior learning through a plethora of metacognitive acts, such as self-reflection (Clark, 2012). The acts of feeding forward and backward oscillate frequently in the midst of students' portfolio compilation processes. Feedback has two major purposes, namely formative and summative ones although teachers should consider making these purposes mutually inclusive rather than mutually exclusive (Lau, 2016). Formative feedback refers to qualitative commentary about learners' strengths and weaknesses. It could be descriptive (performance indexes) and evaluative (comments with rationalisation). Summative feedback appears in the form of letter grades, numerical scores, percentage, or grade point average.

Since most teachers adopt technology in language teaching, the use of computer feedback or electronic feedback (hereafter e-feedback) is commonplace alongside teacher, peer, and self-feedback (Lee, 2017). E-feedback is defined as online or offline feedback information generated by teachers/students through computer-mediated tools or by web-based automatic tools entirely in the second language writing contexts (Ene & Upton, 2018). In digital portfolios, e-feedback has become a regular feature, which promotes students' active agency, independence, metacognitive capacities, learning

DOI: 10.4324/9781003295860-6

motivation, and engagement in writing (Chong, 2017). However, unlike their paper-based counterparts, what makes e-feedback a complex instructional practice in the digital medium is that its implementation is multimodal, hypertextual, synchronous or asynchronous, and reciprocal (i.e. a collective identity shared by students, teachers, peers, and the public), involving in a brand new experience of providing, viewing, interpreting, and responding to those e-feedback messages (Yancey, 2004, 2019). In fact, giving, receiving, and using e-feedback within digital portfolios proficiently require teachers and students alike to have a higher level of computer and assessment literacy, if teachers want to use e-feedback to align writing pedagogy and assessment constructively (Lam, 2021). The next section unpacks the conceptualisation of three feedback perspectives.

Conceptualisation of e-feedback in digital portfolios

In assessment research, scholars have proposed three perspectives of feedback application. They include (1) feedback as a product, (2) feedback as a dialogue, and (3) feedback as an internal driver (Chong, 2019; Espasa et al., 2022). In (1), feedback is considered a message or a gift, which is given from the teacher to their students unilaterally. In this sense, feedback is monologic by nature because it does not involve any negotiations and discussions among the teacher and their students. Such a transmissive view of feedback has its conceptual root in behaviourism in which students are regarded as a passive receiver of knowledge who is expected to rectify their writings with feedback submissively (Sadler, 2010). This static feedback perspective is not likely to promote active agency, learner autonomy, and reflectivity in the portfolio process, given that students are relegated to a faithful follower who simply adopts teacher feedback without thought. When the feedback-as-a-product perspective is contextualised in digital portfolios, e-feedback is mainly given in the written and offline mode through emails, forum messages, or track changes in word processing documents. Although this product-oriented feedback approach does not create interactive dialogues, it remains predominantly adopted in second language writing classrooms due to several reasons, including time efficiency, lack of teacher or student assessment literacy, and deep-seated hierarchical relationships between teachers and students in some cultures (Carless, 2015).

In (2), feedback is likened to a dynamic and dialogic process between the teacher and their students. To this end, feedback takes the form of an ongoing dialogic within and over different units, tasks, and activities. It assumes a mutual, communal, and cooperative relationship among teacher-to-students, students-to-teacher, and students-to-students. Such an organic view of feedback has its conceptual root in socio-constructivism, wherein students are encouraged to actively engage in assessment dialogues with their teacher, peers, as well as themselves (an instance of inner dialogues; Carless & Boud, 2018). This reciprocal feedback perspective is inclined to enhance students' digital portfolio assessment literacy, trust between the teacher and their students, and uptake of assessment information. The rationale for feedback-as-a-dialogue perspective dovetails nicely with the attributes of digital portfolios, which support collaboration, collegiality, and a community of enquiry through a discovery composing approach (Yancey, 2019). When (2) is applied in the digital portfolio environment, e-feedback is generated among the teacher, their students, and peers collectively both online and offline. It could be in multiple formats and media, such as written, audio, or video (Espasa et al., 2022). Nevertheless, it may be easier said than done to introduce the feedback-as-a-dialogue approach in primary and secondary schools because students tend to be reliant or lack sufficient assessment training in internalising useful feedback for text revisions (Lee et al., 2019).

In (3), feedback is regarded as an internal driver, which facilitates self-monitoring and self-regulation of students' writing development. Feedback serves as a catalyst to help students coordinate their cognition, motivation, and behaviours to achieve the set learning goals (Nicol & Macfarlane-Dick, 2006). Closely linked with the idea of socio-constructivism, such a learner-focused and sustainable view of feedback originates from the theory of meta-cognition (Nicol, 2020). It emphasises that students mobilise prior learning, world knowledge, communal resources (i.e. Internet materials), and multimodal feedback on digital portfolios to make sense of learning and create new knowledge in their digital compositions. These internal processes empower students to set goals with success criteria, monitor the goals with e-feedback, reflect upon, and revise their writings accordingly (Andrade & Brookhart, 2016). Situated in an ipsative assessment paradigm, e-feedback is primarily generated by students themselves or by the teacher to close the learning gaps between the students' prior and current writing performances. It may take the form of digital texts (web-blog commentaries) or videos (vlogs on YouTube) as a reflective tool in their portfolios (Law & Baer, 2020). While the feedback-as-an-internal-driver approach is personal, younger or less proficient students may need initial guidance from the teacher to help them self-regulate their learning. The following section details integration of e-feedback into digital portfolios in terms of sources, modes, and types of technologies.

Integration of e-feedback into portfolios

Besides self-feedback, e-feedback has three *sources* in digital portfolios, namely online teacher, peer, and automated feedback. Online teacher feedback provides students with e-feedback through electronic files (i.e. Microsoft Word) and text chats. Its focus usually underscores content more than mechanics although attention is given to linguistic errors as well. Students generally prefer online teacher feedback as compared to handwritten feedback because the former is more detailed, much legible, convenient, and trustworthy (Ene & Upton, 2018). Online peer feedback is relatively easier to create and adopt in virtual learning environments than in face-to-face instructional settings because it is generated much faster and more flexibly through Web 2.0 tools, such as Google Docs. Electronic peer feedback has the following benefits. Students are able to make better text revisions in terms of both local and global concerns. They can upgrade the overall quality of their writings, including improvement in sentence structures, reduction in grammatical errors, and variation in vocabulary choice (Shang, 2022). Despite these promising outcomes, online peer feedback is deemed less constructive, less dependable, and less significant as it mostly addresses lower-order concerns (Chen, 2016). To enhance the usefulness of online peer feedback, students need focused training in giving and enacting peer feedback and learn how to take up different roles as audience, as assistants, and as evaluators in the online peer assessment process. Online automated feedback generates instant comments through automatic writing evaluation systems (e.g. Pigai) and language editing tools (e.g. Grammarly). Students who receive more online automated feedback tend to engage in this feedback source more frequently, produce more text revisions, and obtain higher scores in assessments (Zhu et al., 2020). Although students are likely to adopt online automated feedback tools once they have been introduced, some students remain sceptical about their accuracy and some simply ignore the feedback they generate. It is because they are perplexed about the correct usage of this automated feedback due to an obvious lack of training in how to interpret the feedback in context. Some scholars have suggested that the use of such tools is flagging (Koltovskaia, 2020).

The *modes* of e-feedback occur synchronously (the teacher and students being online simultaneously) and asynchronously (the teacher and students not being online at the same time). They can be represented in the forms of audio, video, and text formats. Audio feedback refers to sound-only feedback stored in MP3 files or audio-recordings downloadable from a podcast. Video feedback refers to screencast feedback, which captures how a student's text is graded against rubrics with the teacher's pre-recorded commentary. A case in point is the use of Jing, a user-friendly screencast feedback tool for writing teachers. The screencast video can be saved as a link and sent back to students via emails (Lee, 2017). Text feedback refers to written corrective feedback displayed in "Track Changes" and "New Comments" of word processing software (e.g. Microsoft Word). The pedagogical benefits of these three *modes* of e-feedback are as follows: audio feedback being more personal, pleasant, holistic, and succinct; video feedback enabling a dialogic process and nurturing a sense of closeness; text feedback equipping students with ability to make effective revisions (Espasa et al., 2022). Although the three e-feedback *modes* are conducive to improved learning, some students prefer audio/video feedback to text feedback, since the former creates a sense of affinity (i.e. social presence) and trust among feedback givers and receivers (Ranalli, 2021). With that said, a majority of students remain favourable to a combination of two to three feedback modes (i.e. video plus text or audio plus text), considering that these eclectic modes are complementary rather than incompatible (Ice et al., 2010).

According to a review of technology and its effectiveness in language learning, Golonka et al. (2014) formulated a six-tier taxonomy with examples. In the taxonomy, each *type* of technology is listed with its corresponding tools to facilitate production of e-feedback. The first *type* is (a) classroom-based technologies, such as interactive whiteboards or learning management systems (e.g. Moodle). The second is (b) individual study tools, namely grammar checkers, corpora, or electronic dictionaries. The third is (c) network-based social computing, like weblogs, Facebook, online gaming, or instant messaging (e.g. WhatsApp). The fourth is (d) mobile and portable devices, including smartphones or tablets. The fifth is (e) cloud-based word processors and shared documents, for instance Google Docs and Microsoft Word. The sixth is (f) is web-based email, such as Gmail. Of these six categories, Loncar et al. (2021, p. 20) found that in their technology-mediated feedback review, (a) the use of multiple technologies ranked top, followed by descending order of popularity, namely (b) individual study tools (Pigai, most popular tool), (c) cloud-based word processors and shared documents (i.e. Google Docs, most popular software), (d) network-based social computing, (e) classroom-based technologies/screencasting, and (f) web-based email. From these findings, the use of multiple technologies indicates that students have exercised active agency to regulate the e-feedback process, namely mobilising and uptaking multimodal feedback with informed decisions. The affordances of individual study tools (e.g. Grammarly) and cloud-based shared documents (e.g. Google Docs) enable students to utilise e-feedback reflectively to improve their writing performances via digital portfolios (Ranalli, 2021; Saeed & Al Qunayeer, 2020). The subsequent section presents how teachers can assist students to promote self-regulated learning with e-feedback.

Techniques to promote self-regulated learning with e-feedback

To facilitate self-regulated learning in writing, e-feedback needs to be formative, dynamic, continuous, and actionable. In digital portfolios, teacher provision of formative e-feedback is likely to foster deeper learning, metacognitive strategies, and self-reflective thinking. These higher-order aspects of skills enable students to make more and better revisions (Lv et al., 2021). With its transparency, instantaneity, and interactiveness, e-feedback has potential to be formative so long as it delivers synchronously. Since e-feedback is multimodal, it aligns with the dialogic view of e-feedback. Teacher online feedback can appear in numerous interactive channels, such as chat texts, forums, and Google Docs, in which teachers can provide immediate responses, clarifications, and conversations with students whenever misunderstandings arise (Chong, 2019). These dialogic interactions are indispensable for cultivating students' self-regulated learning capacities. Besides, teachers may provide e-feedback on a regular basis, given that students need multiple opportunities to learn how to set goals, monitor the goals, and review them independently. Although the idea of self-regulated learning is considered an internal process, external factors like teacher-instructed guidance and peer reviews play a crucial role in enhancing the usefulness of e-feedback over time. After all, co-regulation of learning is part and parcel of the development of students' self-regulated learning when teachers adopt the process writing approach (Allal, 2021). To warrant the self-regulatory attributes of e-feedback, it has to be actionable in general and revisable in particular, so that students can act upon the feedback to upgrade their works-in-progress (Yang, 2016). Through successful uptake of teacher e-feedback, students can transfer this internalised knowledge to another course, another grade level, and another learning context, especially after graduation, say from secondary level to undergraduate level and from local educational settings to overseas study environments (Malecka et al., 2022).

To further contextualise how e-feedback facilitates self-regulated learning, we adopt Chong's (2019) four-step guide on students' dynamic use of e-feedback in a digital portfolio programme as a case scenario. Chong's study investigated the use of e-feedback through Google Docs. The four-step guide includes (1) providing feedback, (2) negotiating feedback, (3) reading feedback, and (4) reacting to feedback. For step (1), teachers provide indirect rather than direct feedback, so that students are expected to think about how to adopt it in their interim and final drafts metacognitively. The focus of feedback can shift from linguistic to content issues to facilitate high-quality revisions, namely the global concerns of writing. Teachers should encourage students to make achievable writing goals in relation to success criteria. Prior to feedback provision, they can debrief students about the learning goals in the assessment criteria, ideally accompanied by exemplars completed by previous cohorts of students or teacher models. After the debriefing, students are likely to have a clearer idea of how to set goals for their electronic entries. For step (2), it is the highlight of the entire e-feedback process, since teachers and students can create productive dialogues around the e-feedback provided to students' digital portfolio entries. The former can explain and clarify unclear feedback points via instant messages (e.g. WeChat and WhatsApp) or chat functions built into learning management systems (e.g. Google Classroom) while the latter can raise questions or queries if they are not able to decipher the e-feedback they have received. In this step, teachers may give greater support to those students who are not certain how to set goals or monitor their writing developments. Digital dialogues are likely to reduce students' learning anxiety because engaging in self-regulated learning could be a daunting endeavour to some less proficient students.

For step (3), students are invited to read teachers' e-feedback thoroughly. Because e-feedback can be more legible and less face-threatening than handwritten feedback, students are more motivated to read and internalise e-feedback to improve their writings. It is found that teachers tend to generate longer and more text-specific feedback in the electronic format (Elola & Oskoz, 2017). In terms of accessibility, students can read teachers' or peers' e-feedback practically anywhere and anytime as long as they have an electronic device and Wi-Fi connection. This e-feedback, be it audio, video, or text, can be permanently saved in cloud-based storage systems for unrestricted retrieval, such as Google Drive. Since students need to mobilise a range of e-reading strategies to browse online feedback, such as looking up unfamiliar words in online dictionaries or cross-checking peer online feedback with automatic feedback, they will become more independent and self-regulated to monitor their composing process. For step (4), students may find it convenient to revise their drafts through word processing software, such as, Google Docs and Microsoft Word. On Google Docs, a hypertext could be easily added, deleted, inserted, or rephrased. Students can make informed decisions to revise their texts based upon peer and teacher online input. While revising, they should review whether their drafts achieved the expected writing goals at the outset, for example use of appropriate vocabulary of a genre. In Microsoft Word and Google Docs, the "Track Changes" function assists students to perform minor edits quickly. To make a substantial revision on the hypertext, students can utilise the copy and paste function to save time and effort. In sum, acting upon e-feedback via digital tools, such as Google Docs and Microsoft Word, can facilitate the procedures of progress monitoring and revision in self-regulated learning (Andrade & Brookhart, 2016).

Another instructional approach which can be adopted to nurture school-level students' self-regulated learning with e-feedback is digital storytelling. This method refers to a digital self-discovery approach, which involves students in applying multimodal media to narrate a personal story, language learning experiences, a scientific report, or a critical reflection on a real-life event individually or in small groups via sharing of e-feedback (Brenner, 2014). Since this approach is continuous, autonomous, technological, and metacognitive, students have ample opportunities to take charge of their learning, to make informed decisions with e-feedback, and to monitor how to achieve their writing goals reflectively (Bai et al., 2021). Digital storytelling is said to combine the old tradition (the conventional genre-based approach) and the new tradition (the new literacies trend, i.e. media and digital literacy) productively to make students' authorial voices get across to viewers more instantly, transparently, and interactively. It further promotes creativity, learner independence, critical thinking skills, basic research skills, composing skills, communication skills, and self-regulated learning capacities through interactive use of e-feedback in the digital story-making processes. The acquisition and uptake of these twenty-first-century soft skills is pedagogically crucial, given that students need to be fully equipped before they proceed to the next stage of their study and professional careers (Law & Baer, 2020).

In conventional face-to-face classroom contexts, students are expected to write a story with these elements – a background, a complication, a series of events, a resolution, and an ending with or without a personal reflection. Prior to composing the genre, students are taught how to master the lexico-grammatical features of narrative. While composing, they are usually asked to write individually and under timed conditions. On occasions, students are neither allowed to talk to one another nor refer back to any external resources like dictionaries or textbooks to warrant fairness (Lam, 2018). Nonetheless, when students are assigned to create their digital storytelling projects online, they have greater flexibility and autonomy to make significant decisions from script writing, storyboard design, selection of digital tools, project duration, to means of interactions with peers and the teacher (Lee, 2017). The inclusion of audio (Podcast), video (YouTube), and graphic (the SlideShare presentation website, www.slideshare.net/) components into the project can draw readers' attention more directly and convey the key message of the digital story, for example a soul-searching moral lesson or a life-changing experience more compellingly, provided that the multimodal nature of digital stories can capture students' thinking, facial expressions, emotions, and body language in a remarkably truthful manner (Girmen et al., 2019).

Besides the aforementioned technical aspects, digital storytelling tasks are likely to enhance students' self-regulated learning skills by way of iterative e-feedback. At different stages of the storytelling production, students can practise goal-setting, progress-monitoring, as well as reflection-plus-revising. The following is an illustrative example.

A Grade 8 student with average English proficiency plans to produce a digital story about her three-week immersion trip to Singapore. During the stages of script writing and storyboard design, the student is able to set plans on how to narrate this intriguing language learning experience with regard to the assessment rubrics. When creating the script, the student may consider utilising various types of modalities, like still/motion pictures, audio-recordings, and video clips to be shot in Singapore. Prior to actual production, the student can make a review of whether all multimodal artefacts can attract readers' (the teacher, peers, parents, and principals) attention. At this pre-production stage, the student could elicit peer and teacher e-feedback, so that she can make necessary changes to the script and the storyboard. The student may *record* and then *review* the rehearsal of a preliminary digital story (e.g. a shorter version of the original) and see what could be further improved. When the whole digital storytelling production is near completion, the student is encouraged to perform self-reflection by checking against the assessment rubrics or set goals to make the last-minute edits to mispronunciations (if any), sequence of pictorial presentation, adjustment of volume in the audio files, colour contrast in the visuals, and so on.

As said, the whole digital storytelling process supports students' development of self-regulated learning skills by generating and sharing e-feedback, such as self-assessment, peer review, and self-reflection. Further, digital storytelling is technologically compatible to be parts of a digital portfolio project. Digital storytelling files, apps, and software can be conveniently attached to digital portfolio platforms as one of the hyperlinks or files in the cloud-based drive, depending on what tools students adopt for their digital portfolios. There are user-friendly tools to facilitate the production of basic digital storytelling, including presentation software (e.g. PowerPoint) inserted with audio and video clips or book creation tools, such as My Story Book Maker (an easy-to-use tool: www.mystorybook.com/) and Pictello (an interactive app made by Assistive Ware: www.assistiveware.com/products/pictello). My Story Book Maker is appropriate for younger learners, namely Grades 1–3 under the guidance of teachers and parents. PowerPoint and Pictello may suit upper primary-level students because the software tools involve a higher level of digital literacy skills. The next section is a discussion task, which encourages readers to ponder over the formative potential of e-feedback when applied in digital portfolio environments.

Discussion task

In pairs, discuss the following questions:

1 What is the role of feedback in portfolio assessment? How does e-feedback enhance writing instruction via the digital portfolio approach? Please give two examples to supplement your response.

2 Which perspective of e-feedback application (feedback as a product; feedback as a dialogue; feedback as an internal drive) best describes a vast majority of writing classroom-based assessment practices in L1 and L2 contexts? Explain your answers.
3 Why do some students prefer online teacher feedback to online peer feedback? If your future students do not like online peer feedback, how would you convince them to provide and receive online peer feedback for revision more frequently?
4 In your opinion, which mode of e-feedback (audio, video, text) do you think works best to promote students' writing improvement? Share your standpoints with a classroom example.
5 If you plan to use Google Docs in your e-portfolio programme, what function(s) do you think are most appropriate to optimise students' engagement in editing and revising their digital texts? Please elaborate.
6 Although the digital storytelling approach has been found to be effective in enhancing students' motivation and metacognition, what challenges do you anticipate when teachers introduce this instructional approach with their upper primary students?

Conclusion

Chapter 5 outlined the role of feedback in portfolio assessment and in digital portfolios. The chapter went on to unpack the conceptualisation of e-feedback from three perspectives, namely feedback as a product, feedback as a dialogue, and feedback as an internal driver. It discussed how teachers incorporated e-feedback into digital portfolios by way of different sources, modes, and technology types. Further, the chapter introduced a four-step guide to instruct how teachers could support students' self-regulated learning through applying e-feedback dialogically and metacognitively, followed by an example to illustrate the use of digital storytelling approach in a primary-level school context. Chapter 5 ended with a discussion task, which motivates readers to think more deeply about the learning-oriented potential of e-feedback in digital portfolios.

References

Allal, L. (2021). Involving primary school students in the co-construction of formative assessment in support of writing. *Assessment in Education: Principles, Policy & Practice, 28*(5–6), 584–601.
Andrade, H., & Brookhart, S. M. (2016). The role of classroom assessment in supporting self-regulated learning. In D. Laveault & L. Allal (Eds.), *Assessment for learning: Meeting the challenge of implementation* (pp. 293–309). Springer.

Bai, B., Wang, J., & Zhou, H. (2021). An intervention study to improve primary school students' self-regulated strategy use in English writing through e-learning in Hong Kong. *Computer Assisted Language Learning*. https://doi.org/10.1080/09588221.2020.1871030

Brenner, K. (2014). Digital stories: A 21st century communication tool for the English language classroom. *English Teaching Forum*, *52*(1), 22–29.

Carless, D. (2015). *Excellence in university assessment: Learning from award-winning practice*. Routledge.

Carless, D., & Boud, D. (2018). The development of student feedback literacy: Enabling uptake of feedback. *Assessment & Evaluation in Higher Education*, *43*(8), 1315–1325.

Chen, T. (2016). Technology-supported peer feedback in ESL/EFL writing classes: A research synthesis. *Computer Assisted Language Learning*, *29*(2), 365–397.

Chong, I. (2017). Assessment dialogues between teachers and students in e-writing portfolios. *TESOL Journal*, *8*(1), 240–243.

Chong, S. W. (2019). College students' perception of e-feedback: A grounded theory perspective. *Assessment & Evaluation in Higher Education*, *44*(7), 1090–1105.

Clark, I. (2012). Formative assessment: Assessment is for self-regulated learning. *Educational Psychology Review*, *24*(2), 205–249.

Elola, I., & Oskoz, A. (2017). Writing with 21st century social tools in the L2 classroom: New literacies, genres, and writing practices. *Journal of Second Language Writing*, *36*, 52–60.

Ene, E., & Upton, T. A. (2018). Synchronous and asynchronous teacher electronic feedback and learner uptake in ESL composition. *Journal of Second Language Writing*, *41*, 1–13.

Espasa, A., Mayordomo, R. M., Guasch, T., & Martinez-Melo, M. (2022). Does the type of feedback channel used in online learning environments matter? Students' perceptions and impact on learning. *Active Learning in Higher Education*, *23*(1), 49–63.

Girmen, P., Özkanal, Ü, & Dayan, G. (2019). Digital storytelling in the language arts classroom. *Universal Journal of Educational Research*, *7*(1), 55–65.

Golonka, E. W., Bowles, A. R., Frank, V. M., Richardson, D. L., & Freynik, S. (2014). Technologies for foreign language learning: A review of technology types and their effectiveness. *Computer Assisted Language Learning*, *27*(1), 70–105.

Ice, P., Swan, K., Diaz, S., Kupczynski, L., & Swan-Dagen, A. (2010). An analysis of students' perceptions of the value and efficacy of instructors' auditory and text-based feedback modalities across multiple conceptual levels. *Journal of Educational Computing Research*, *43*(1), 113–134.

Koltovskaia, S. (2020). Student engagement with automated written corrective feedback (AWCF) provided by Grammarly: A multiple case study. *Assessing Writing*, *44*, 100450.

Lam, R. (2018). Teacher learning of portfolio assessment practices: Testimonies of two writing teachers. In H. Jiang & M. F. Hill (Eds.), *Teacher learning from classroom assessment: Perspectives from Asia Pacific* (pp. 99–118). Springer.

Lam, R. (2021). Using ePortfolios to promote assessment of, for, as learning in EFL writing. *The European Journal of Applied Linguistics and TEFL*, *10*(1), 101–120.

Lau, A. M. Z. (2016). "Formative good, summative bad?" – A review of the dichotomy in assessment literature. *Journal of Further and Higher Education, 40*(4), 509–525.

Law, S., & Baer, A. (2020). Using technology and structured peer reviews to enhance students' writing. *Active Learning in Higher Education, 21*(1), 23–38.

Lee, I. (2017). *Classroom writing assessment and feedback in L2 school contexts.* Springer.

Lee, I., Mak, P., & Yuan, R. (2019). Assessment as learning in primary writing classrooms: An exploratory study. *Studies in Educational Evaluation, 62*, 72–81.

Loncar, M., Schams, W., & Liang, J. (2021). Multiple technologies, multiple sources: Trends and analyses of the literature on technology-mediated feedback for L2 English writing published from 2015–2019. *Computer Assisted Language Learning.* https://doi.org/10.1080/09588221.2021.1943452

Lv, X., Ren, W., & Xie, Y. (2021). The effects of online feedback on ESL/EFL writing: A meta-analysis. *The Asia-Pacific Education Researcher, 30*(6), 643–653.

Malecka, B., Boud, D., Tai, J., & Ajjawi, R. (2022). Navigating feedback practices across learning contexts: Implications for feedback literacy. *Assessment & Evaluation in Higher Education.* https://doi.org/10.1080/02602938.2022.2041544

Nicol, D. (2020). The power of internal feedback: Exploiting natural comparison processes. *Assessment & Evaluation in Higher Education, 46*(5), 756–778.

Nicol, D., & Macfarlane-Dick, D. (2006). Formative assessment and self-regulated learning: A model and seven principles of good feedback practice. *Studies in Higher Education, 31*(2), 199–218.

Ranalli, J. (2021). L2 student engagement with automated feedback on writing: Potential for learning and issues of trust. *Journal of Second Language Writing, 52*, 100816.

Sadler, D. R. (2010). Beyond feedback: Developing student capability in complex appraisal. *Assessment & Evaluation in Higher Education, 35*(5), 535–550.

Saeed, M. A., & Al Qunayeer, H. S. (2020). Exploring teacher interactive e-feedback on students' writing through Google Docs: Factors promoting interactivity and potential for learning. *The Language Learning Journal.* https://doi.org/10.1080/09571736.2020.1786711

Shang, H. F. (2022). Exploring online peer feedback and automated corrective feedback on EFL writing performance. *Interactive Learning Environments, 30*(1), 4–16.

Yancey, K. B. (2004). Postmodernism, palimpsest, and portfolios: Theoretical issues in the representation of student work. *College Composition and Communication, 55*(4), 738–761.

Yancey, K. B. (Ed.). (2019). *ePortfolio as curriculum: Models and practices for developing students' ePortfolio literacy.* Stylus Publishing.

Yang, Y. (2016). Transforming and constructing academic knowledge through online peer feedback in summary writing. *Computer Assisted Language Learning, 29*(4), 683–702.

Zhu, M., Liu, O. L., & Lee, H. S. (2020). The effect of automated feedback on revision behavior and learning gains in formative assessment of scientific argument writing. *Computers & Education, 143*, 103668.

6 Digital Portfolio Application Tools

Overview of digital portfolio tools

Nowadays, people from all walks of life use electronic gadgets every day, everywhere, and at all times owing to the popularity of portable, handheld, mobile technologies, such as smartphones and tablets. Learners are no exception. The majority of students in most contexts around the world will have access to an Internet-enabled device and can, therefore, engage in technology-enabled learning. Indeed, when technology is appropriately integrated into the language curriculum, it can be pedagogically fun, engaging, and fulfilling (Navarre, 2019). Common digital tools designed for educational purposes (or e-learning tools), such as Kahoot and Nearpod, can be used to develop student autonomy, create a sense of curiosity, and nurture a community of practice through students' active participation. Technically speaking, as they are designed for learning, these digital tools are user-friendly, and aesthetically pleasing, which could accommodate diverse students' learning needs (Armstrong & Armstrong, 2022). More importantly, most of these digital tools have tablet, mobile apps, and web-based versions, which make them even more accessible, functional, and emancipating.

Since the turn of the century, the Ministries of Education in various jurisdictions have implemented educational reforms, which promoted learner-centred curricula (e.g. project-based learning), alternative pedagogical approaches (e.g. process writing), and extensive use of e-assessment (e.g. digital portfolios) to synergise teaching and assessment constructively. Take digital portfolios as an illustrative example; about 20 years ago, digital portfolio was in the form of word processor and presentation software files uploaded on floppy discs or perspective school portals, that is intranet (Yancey, 2004). Nevertheless, in the last decade, a plethora of open-source learning management systems and customised digital portfolio software tools were developed owing to educational, technological, and commercial demands (Lam, 2021). Learning management systems include Moodle,

DOI: 10.4324/9781003295860-7

Blackboard, Mahara, Padlet, and Canvas, whereas digital portfolio software entails Blogger, Seesaw, Schoology, and FreshGrade. Of these tools, some will be further reviewed and discussed in the subsequent sections. In parallel with constructivist educational philosophies, the advent of these e-learning and digital portfolio applications can help teachers support students' acquisition of the twenty-first-century study skills, including critical thinking skills, metacognitive skills, and communication skills, which equip students with lifelong learning capacity beyond their study careers (Russell & Murphy-Judy, 2021). The next section unfolds the rationale behind these digital portfolio applications.

Rationale behind the use of digital portfolio applications

Unlike their print counterparts, digital portfolio applications transcend time, space, and modality effortlessly. Restricted by physical size, paper-based portfolios can be easily misplaced, mismanaged, or even disappear as students move through their schooling. With digital portfolios, teachers can assist students to connect the prior, current, and future learning of writing seamlessly, enabling students' knowledge transfer and creation with regard to multimodal artefacts on various e-learning platforms, such as Google Classroom or customised digital application tools, such as Seesaw. To learn and improve writing, students can rely on commercial digital portfolio applications to help them create initial drafts and storyboards, draw on various online resources (built-in library or dictionary), reflect on journals and evidence of learning, and coordinate collaborative writing activities like peer editing (Shaban & Abobaker, 2022). These functionalities of digital portfolio applications can broaden students' learning strategies and repertoire. In the following, I discuss the tripartite rationale behind the use of everyday digital portfolio applications as adapted from Hand et al. (2012).

Personalised learning

Using digital portfolio applications, students can enjoy autonomy and privacy denied to them in teacher-centred writing classrooms. In those settings, students are reduced to passive learners who learn how to write by mimicking specific genre structures and lexico-grammatical features. When students compose their writings in digital portfolios, they develop their own individual styles as well as an independent learner identity, for instance, relying on extensive use of visuals and graphics to help them express their ideas three-dimensionally. More importantly, students can keep their learning artefacts confidential because digital portfolios provide students with a personal platform which solely belongs to them, especially when enabled with a password-protected login. Digital portfolios take learning writing to a whole new level by granting students freedom to customise their portfolios and enabling them to transfer portfolio contents across grade levels, subjects, and even institutions, so that they have a fuller sense of agency, authorship, and locus of control in their learning journeys.

Reflective learning

Metacognition is the key to writing instruction. One main takeaway of adopting digital portfolio applications is to encourage students to partake in setting goals, monitoring goals, reflecting on goals, and updating composing skills in accordance with the set goals. Students can engage in reflective learning in digital portfolios, which expect them to compile, curate, reflect on, and revise their works-in-progress while developing their e-portfolios. By assisting students to reflect on their evidence of learning, they are asked to keep a digital journal, in which they are provided with some pointers or guided questions to ponder over the quality of their completed and ongoing written tasks uploaded on digital portfolios. To facilitate the acts of reflection, students can explore other modalities when they review their portfolio contents, namely audio, video, or digital photos to accommodate their learning needs. Since reflective learning is a central element in digital portfolios, application tools with this metacognitive function are preferred.

Collaborative learning

Besides a personal learning environment, most digital portfolio applications support collaborative learning by default. Collaborative writing enhances students' self-efficacy, confidence, writing performance, and critical thinking skills, especially through peer assessment (Storch, 2019). Socially, students can utilise digital portfolio applications to make friends, both locally (within the same school) and internationally (friends from short-term immersion programmes or multiplayer online games). Pedagogically, teachers may encourage students to compile an intercultural digital portfolio, which investigates New Year celebrations in different parts of Asia together with their online friends, for instance, Diwali in India and Songkran in Thailand. Technologically, students may develop this unique digital portfolio by way of an online word processor like Google Docs and weblogs like Blogger, which feature collaborative writing, peer editing, and academic publishing. In face-to-face instruction, teachers can also adopt a digital portfolio application to monitor how students work on their portfolio tasks in groups and how they peer evaluate their groupmates as parts of summative assessment. The following section discusses selection criteria when teachers choose prospective portfolio tools for use.

Criteria for selecting appropriate portfolio tools

When choosing the right application, teachers need to take two aspects into account, namely (1) learners and (2) tools (Navarre, 2019). For learners, we subdivide this aspect into (a) learner digital literacy, (b) age, and (c) individual differences. For tools, we break down the second aspect into (a) purpose of instructional technology and (b) levels of technology integration. Concerning (1a), teachers need to take student level of digital literacy into consideration when selecting a tool. Although learners of new generation were born in a digital era and are unanimously called digital natives, it does not necessarily mean that they can manipulate instructional tools effectively. It goes without saying that students use smartphones, send emails, surf the Internet for entertainment, and play online games rather proficiently. However, research has shown that students, when engaged in online educational tasks, found it challenging to overcome certain basic technical issues, such as converting Word files into PDF versions for uploading and formatting word processed assignments (Johnson & Kawasaki, 2017). In addition, students may not develop strong awareness of online identity, privacy, and cybersecurity because they are usually too young to guard against these aspects. Hence, teachers may provide students with an induction programme prior to the full adoption of a new digital portfolio tool. Alternatively, students can be asked to watch a tutorial video on a video-hosting site, such as YouTube, of that application tool before they have hands-on experience.

As to (1b), when teachers select digital portfolio applications for their students, age is a key factor. The National Association for the Education of Young Children published a web-based document, which classifies learners into three age groups when technology and media are applied, including infants and toddlers, pre-schoolers and kindergarteners, and school-age children. Take second graders as example, they like to draw pictures, talk about themselves, and play around with stationeries. They may have developed fine motor skills for handwriting but not for keyboarding since the latter demands much more hand–eye coordination and frequent practice. Teachers may go for a tablet-optimised app version of a digital tool, so that these young learners can use the touchscreen function by dragging and dropping objects on the interface rather than keyboarding their portfolio tasks. Further, selecting a digital portfolio application with more colourful and cartoon icons will enhance student motivation to engage in portfolio tasks, such as Seesaw (https://web.seesaw.me/; Moorhouse, 2019; Moorhouse & Beaumont, 2020).

As regards (1c), teachers need to respect and accommodate individual differences, especially when students have diverse learning styles, such as visual, aural, scholastic, and kinaesthetic ones. Besides picking the right tool, teachers may involve students in the decision-making process by considering the modality (audio, video, and text), the medium (synchronous or asynchronous), and the content (narratives or expository) to be presented in their digital portfolio platforms to showcase their best writing performances. Teachers also ensure whether the selected digital portfolio tool emphasises learner autonomy and use of multimodal functions, for instance easy upload of video and sound files as evidence of learning for self-reflection. Some digital tools that can be used for digital portfolio compiling are relatively prescriptive, denying students' opportunity and autonomy to take charge of their learning. Portfolio applications that put students at the centre of learning and address individual differences can become teachers' first priority.

Regarding (2a), the purpose of instructional technology should align with teachers' educational philosophies and curriculum design. If teachers wish to enhance teacher–student and student–student interactions, they may integrate Quizlet (https://quizlet.com/) games into their digital portfolio programmes, because this app encourages peer competition, social learning (especially in teams), and active participation. Another case in point is that if teachers believe developing young learners' literacy skills is of utmost importance, they may utilise web-blogs (WordPress; https://wordpress.com/) as the digital portfolio tool. On web-blogs, students can share their extensive reading in writing, compose their post-reading reflection as blog posts, and invite peers and the teacher to leave comments. Besides, if teachers have already adopted a process-oriented approach to writing instruction, they may choose Google Docs or Wiki as part of formative writing tasks. These two electronic tools allow learners to draft and redraft their writings in stages and to facilitate the uptake of peer feedback at learners' fingertips.

Speaking of technology integration (2b), teachers are advised to evaluate the effectiveness of digital portfolio applications by the SAMR model, in which S stands for substitution, A augmentation, M modification, and R redefinition (Puentedura, 2014). The first two levels target lesser enhancement of existing pedagogy through technology integration, namely from no change to minor functional change, whereas the last two aim at transforming language instruction more substantially, like an overhaul from grammar-based writing tasks to synchronous collaborative writing tasks (see Figure 6.1). According to Navarre (2019), the advantage of the SAMR model is that not only do teachers assess the usefulness of digital portfolio implementations with the model, but they also develop a better understanding of how a digital portfolio tool could alter how teachers deliver instruction more dynamically (sharing of responsibility with students) and how

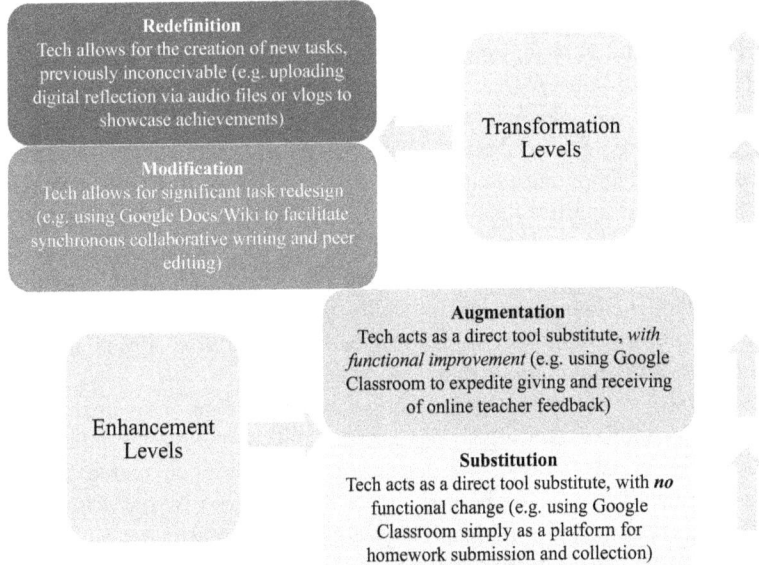

Figure 6.1 SAMR Model and Digital Portfolio Integration
Source: adapted from Puentedura, 2014.

students learn more independently (increase in learner agency in the portfolio process). The subsequent section introduces three common types of digital portfolios in detail.

Three common types of digital portfolios

Renwick (2017) has categorised digital portfolios into three common types, including (a) blogs, (b) customised portfolio applications, and (c) websites. Blogs belong to open-source common tools (e.g. Blogger and WordPress); customised portfolio applications refer to open-source digital portfolio software (e.g. FreshGrade and Seesaw); and websites are about average commercial web-based software (e.g. Wix and Weebly; Stefani et al., 2007). Renwick (2017) added that there were two underlying principles to guide how teachers adopted these three common digital portfolio applications. First, writing instruction, not technology, is a priority. Second, the digital portfolio tool must fit the pedagogy. These principles dovetail nicely with the selection criteria for appropriate portfolio applications – (2a) in the previous section.

Blogs

Blogs are an online space for learners to share about their opinions and feelings on different topics, including diary entries, poems, short stories, playscripts, and travelogues. These digital media facilitate mutual communications between bloggers who create blog posts and virtual viewers who respond to the posts publicly. Blogs are designed for publishing students' works in a wider online community. They allow students to compile, curate, reflect on, and upgrade their in- and out-of-class assignments and personal writings throughout their schooling. Blogs are considered the most basic and easiest version among other digital portfolio applications, and they target the development of literacy skills, yet teachers may encourage students to nurture their oracy skills by uploading either audio files on the blog entries as a brief audiobook or a podcast episode.

The basic features of a blog entail pages (for creating individual entry), categories and tags (for organising entries), and comments (for online peer feedback). In the market, today, there are a plethora of open-source, free-to-use, applications, such as Blogger (www.blogger.com), WordPress (www.wordpress.com), and Edublogs (www.edublogs.org). Blogger and WordPress can be used with senior form students since the tools require more keyboarding skills, whereas Edublogs are intended for junior pupils who still need teachers' and parents' assistance when inputting their works on the blogging sites. The pros of using blogs as digital portfolios include getting connected with wider audiences, having an easier start, and allowing timely peer response. The cons involve infringing students' privacy if a closed account is not used and demanding too many fine motor skills (acts of keyboarding) and too much visibility (largely letter recognition) from young learners.

Customised portfolio applications

Customised portfolio applications refer to personalised, web-based portfolio tools, which help students to take stock of their learning. These applications tend to be accessible, user-friendly, and communal. Students can easily upload their multimodal artefacts of learning, such as audio, video, text, and graphics on these platforms. Once uploaded, the tools have a notification function, which alerts both teachers and parents. Because of this, teachers and guardians can monitor students' mastery performance and academic growth almost at a glance. The principle of these tools is to capture students' learning profiles and enhance their virtual interactions with teachers and parents. There are two popular customised portfolio applications in education, namely Seesaw (https://web.seesaw.me/) and FreshGrade (www.freshgrade.com). Both applications target K-12 learners although they are more suitable for primary-level students.

Take Seesaw, for example, its functions include posting students' works and teachers' lesson plans, assigning class activities, and sending announcements. Its main purpose is to track students' learning progress formatively. Other instructional functions consist of a class blog to facilitate giving and receiving peer and parent feedback and a recordable whiteboard for remote instruction. Seesaw can be readily accessed via a web browser or an app. It has a free-of-charge version (for students, teachers, and parents) and two subscription plans, namely Seesaw Plus (for individual teachers) and Seesaw School (a full version for schools and districts). The benefits of Seesaw include user-friendliness, connectivity with parents, and requirement of low technological skills, whereas its drawbacks entail the lack of a summative evaluation function (a built-in grade book) and limited sustainability to transfer learning data beyond K-12. The in-class and family application of Seesaw (via an app for parents) will be further discussed in Chapter 7, Vignette 1.

Websites

Web-based digital portfolios are about creation of a portfolio via free or paid website builders, namely Google Sites (www.sites.google.com/new) and Wix (www.wix.com/). These website builders are predesigned with a range of pages, templates, banners, themes, and logos. After induction programmes or YouTube tutorials, students are expected to construct their web-based portfolios autonomously. These web-based portfolio sites allow students to copy and paste, drag and drop, and retrieve documents or other artefacts just a stone's throw from cloud-based drives. Their purpose is to promote creativity, learner independence, and lifelong learning. Because these websites are typically permanent, students are likely to keep track of their writing trajectories over time. The portfolio contents could cover interdisciplinary, intercultural, and multilingual topics supported by hyperlinks, online databases, and pop-up menus.

Web-based portfolios are more appropriate for senior students as the required level of digital literacy is higher. In its latest version, the new Google Sites has become more user-friendly with its interface, usability, and connectivity. The new version makes portfolio management easier since there was an overhaul of its interface. It has a preview function, in which students can preview draft and published versions of their webpages. The new Google Sites is also mobile-friendly, adjusting the best configuration for tablets, mobiles, and desktops seamlessly. The advantage of adopting web-based portfolios is that students can enjoy a fuller sense of digital presence, since they construct their digital portfolios from scratch. Another merit is about increased visibility because web-based portfolios can reach more viewers. The shortcomings include fewer opportunities to communicate with parents and more complicated skills in maintaining portfolios. The subsequent section presents a review of three digital portfolio tools.

A review of digital portfolio software

In the following, we evaluate three common digital portfolio software tools separately. They include (1) Google Workspace for Education (formerly G Suite for Education), (2) ClassDojo, and (3) FreshGrade. Under each subsection, we have attached a hyperlink to the online YouTube tutorial of that portfolio software.

> *Google Workspace for Education* (https://edu.google.com/products/workspace-for-education/)
> Tutorial of Google Classroom: www.youtube.com/watch?v=jRP2oIolaaM

Google Workspace for Education is part of a larger Google service, which contains multiple web-based tools to facilitate remote instruction and e-learning in our everyday lives. Dissimilar to other course management systems, Google Workspace has a suite of interactive and collaborative Google apps, which are freely available to students, teachers, parents, and districts for educational use. These Google apps can be browsed and used on webs, mobiles, and tablets. Google Workspace is one of the most popular digital portfolio applications among primary-level and secondary-level schools worldwide. Because of convenient accessibility, easy start-up, and diverse functionalities, Google Workspace requires a minimal digital competency when in use. Although Google Workspace was not originally designed to be an all-in-one learning management system, it increasingly is heading in this direction, especially during the COVID-19 pandemic. Google Workspace consists of Google Classroom, Google Forms, Google Keep, Google Calendar, Gmail, Google Meet, Google Docs/Sheets/Slides, Jamboard, and Google Drive. We outline the functions of selected electronic tools for teacher/readers' consideration.

- *Google Classroom*: It is a core hub of Google Workspace, which connects to other apps. Teachers can set up courses and publish course information (title, course ID, syllabus, instructional materials, and assessment tasks) via the app. After logging in, students can join their respective classes by course ID. The digital platform is used for assignment submission and collection. Students can receive peer and teacher feedback in their Google Classroom.

- *Google Forms*: It is one of the interactive web applications, which allow learners to create, edit, and revise online surveys in real time. Teachers can use the tool as an assessment data bank to house online quizzes, homework assignments, and worksheets. Because Google Forms is also in sync with other Google apps, the outcomes of students' online quizzes are automatically generated and sent to the teacher's Gmail account as well as saved in her Google Drive for review, analysis, and record-keeping.
- *Google Keep*: It is a note-taking app, which helps students organise their schoolworks, class schedules, and extracurricular activities in a methodical way. The app features image-to-text and speech-to-text transcriptions, which take note-taking to the next level. The app can transform text notes into checklists for easy viewing. These text notes can easily be copied to Google Docs and Slides with a built-in button. Google Keep also allows note-taking by voice, which accommodates students with special education needs.
- *Google Meet* (formerly Hangouts): This app is an instant messaging plus videoconferencing application, like Zoom or Skype. It can be used for online audio/video lectures by inviting up to 100 attendees for 60 minutes free. In its latest version, it has a breakout room function, which facilitates small-group interactions designated by the host.
- *Google Docs, Sheets, and Slides*: These apps are equivalent to the counterparts of Word, Excel, and PowerPoint in the Microsoft Office Suite. Since these application tools are web-only, they allow multiple users to create, edit, revise, and share with different people synchronously.
- *Google Jamboard*: Google Jamboard is a digital interactive whiteboard, promoting collaborative writing and group drawing in real time. Jamboard can be used with Google Docs, Sheets, Slides, and Google Drive to facilitate cross-referencing, source text borrowing, and image retrieving. Thus, the Jamboard contents can be frequently modified, edited, and revised before they are presented in front of classmates, parents, and the teacher via Meet or Zoom.

Pros: Google Workspace is flexible, powerful, and learning-oriented, which suits remote instruction well enough. It is free-of-charge and easy to register. Teachers can start their digital portfolio applications according to specific pedagogical needs, for instance introduction of collaborative writing and peer assessment in the online lectures. With Workspace, teachers may not need additional IT support.

Cons: Google Workspace is not recommended for young learners aged between 3 and 6 as some apps involve complex keyboarding skills. This digital portfolio tool does not emphasise communication with parents, nor does it include a proper summative grading option.

ClassDojo (www.classdojo.com/)
Tutorial: www.youtube.com/watch?v=oufeciODPuo&t=39s

ClassDojo is an online classroom management system, where teachers can record and track student behaviours, facilitate classroom activities, check on students' portfolios, and promote home–school communications. Since 2012, it has been widely adopted in school settings in North America, Europe, and Australia. The app aims to promote students' growth mindset and enhances empathy. It has three versions for students, teachers, and parents with a key focus on school–parent communication. All three versions are free. The platform can be accessed on most electronic gadgets, such as tablets, smartphones, and apps. Students and parents log in the tool by a QR code, a text code, or a web browser like Chrome. ClassDojo mainly targets K-6 students. Senior year students may find ClassDojo somewhat restrictive and perhaps unfulfilling. Since its major purpose is to capture and document students' learning growth and classroom behaviours over time, ClassDojo is considered a progressive digital portfolio.

ClassDojo has four tabs in its front dashboard, including *Classroom*, *Portfolios*, *School Story*, and *Messages*. *Classroom* is used to manage students' profiles in a class. *Portfolios* serve to share instructional materials with parents, such as pictures, video, writings, or voice recordings, so that they know how their children are learning in school. Students can upload homework assignments on the app and download learning materials. Once students' works are endorsed and published in *Portfolios*, parents and teachers can leave comments. *School Story* disseminates school-wide updates and activities, whereas *Messages* enable teachers to set quiet hours, download history of messages, and send messages to multiple parents in one go. There are two unique functions of ClassDojo. First, teachers can award points for students' positive classroom behaviours to ensure effectual classroom management. This function helps monitor students' personal development other than their academic performances. Another new function is Conundrums, where the tool presents a range of issue-based scenarios for students to resolve together with their peers, parents, and the teacher. This function nurtures students' critical thinking and problem-solving skills.

Pros: ClassDojo has a fancy and colourful template, which is appealing to young learners. Its interface is also easy to manage. The digital tool has a powerful translation function, which supports up to 36 languages, including traditional Chinese, simplified Chinese, Japanese, Korean, Spanish, and

Digital Portfolio Application Tools 77

so on. Teachers and parents can break the language barrier if they want to communicate with their counterparts in other countries.

Cons: Privacy is always a concern, especially when students' classroom behaviour data are made public. The app lacks built-in instructional data bank like lesson plans, worksheets, and e-books. Teachers need to create and upload all their lesson materials on the platform. In addition, the tool appears to focus more on students' classroom behaviours than on their academic achievements (i.e. students' portfolios).

FreshGrade (https://freshgrade.com/)
Tutorial: www.youtube.com/watch?v=NJsJxhYKyBI&t=9s

FreshGrade is an online portfolio tool, which features dynamic interaction among students, parents, and teachers. The digital tool allows users to leave comment on students' schoolworks, so that students can get timely feedback from peers, parents, and/or teachers. Teachers can upload flipped learning materials, link other instructional resources, and select most appropriate assessment tasks with regard to the school-based curriculum and students' learning needs. Unlike other digital portfolio applications, FreshGrade is a tool that includes a summative assessment function by default. The portfolio software has a range of assessment types to choose from, namely letter grades, total points, percentage, criterion-referenced rubrics, and anecdotal descriptions (Renwick, 2017). The fundamental functions of FreshGrade are free for all users, but its advanced version requires monthly subscription from school. Except for its unique gradebook feature, FreshGrade is similar to Seesaw in terms of purpose, function, and target audience, such as showcasing and celebrating students' learning with family members in a digital medium.

FreshGrade has three components on its dashboard, namely *Class Feed*, *Portfolio*, and *Assessment*. *Class Feed* facilitates sending and receiving messages and announcements among stakeholders, records all learning and teaching events for parents' reference, and promotes constructive dialogues to communicate how students learn in school. *Portfolio* is a core element, which enables students to upload multimodal artefacts for showcasing their writing ability. Each student user has their own personalised digital portfolio with a learning journal. Because of its straightforward interface, FreshGrade allows students to customise their portfolio views by labelling, sorting, and filtering readily. *Assessment* is a highlighted feature of the tool because FreshGrade has a powerful gradebook, which assists teachers to perform standards-based, score-based, or narrative-based assessments. More importantly, summative assessment results notify students and parents promptly to keep them informed. The *Assessment* page can align assessment tasks with standards and learning objectives pedagogically. It also promotes formative assessment by inviting students to focus on how they can improve their learning via e-assessment data.

Pros: With its gradebook and learning portfolios, FreshGrade has potential to engage students in deep learning, such as self-reflection. Because the digital portfolio tool emphasises students' academic achievements, teachers can carry out a broad range of assessment activities with and for students, such as reflective journaling, digital portfolio analysis, and peer coaching to maximise students' digital presence and active agency through its *Portfolio* page.

Cons: Despite its user-friendly interface, FreshGrade may not be as attractive as its counterparts, like ClassDojo. Since FreshGrade has individual portfolios for each student, the tool is best for fifth graders and above. Young learners may find it demanding to compile their portfolios independently although FreshGrade targets K-12 students. The other drawback is that FreshGrade is not compatible with other learning management systems, as it adopts a stand-alone model by its company.

Mini-research task

Study the lesson plan shown in Table 6.1 carefully. The lesson plan was taken from a scheme of work when remote teaching was delivered during the fifth wave of the COVID-19 pandemic in Hong Kong. It is provided by an in-service English teacher, working in one Hong Kong secondary school with English as the medium of instruction. Over 85% of the students in this school belong to top-scorers in the territory. While you are reading the lesson plan, please ponder over the following aspects:

- Teaching topic
- Language focus (specific language skills taught)
- Sequence of instructional steps
- Digital application tools utilised in lessons
- To what extent these online tools can be further maximised

After your reflection, complete a mini-research task on how you can utilise a suite of Google tools listed in Table 6.1 to plan a process-oriented, collaborative writing lesson with a topic on cyberbullying. You are encouraged to explore other online application tools whenever you deem it appropriate. While doing the task, you may consider the following pointers:

- Functionality
- Pedagogical purpose
- Unique features
- Compatibility with other apps/tools
- Pros and cons

Table 6.1 Lesson plan

Background:
The COVID-19 pandemic has hugely destabilised the education sector in recent years. The emergent transition from face-to-face to online learning has significantly disrupted students' learning opportunities worldwide. It has become increasingly crucial for frontline educators to utilise online learning resources effectively, create an interactive, engaging, and systematic remote learning space for learners to thrive, and cater to their diverse learning needs, even at home.
This unit is about shopping and overspending. Students are introduced to the topic of responsible buying. They are expected to acquire knowledge about responsible shopping and impulse buying by reading a blog entry titled *Impulse buying – why do we do it?* This reading practice offers students illuminating insight into the follow-up writing task, a speech about students' impulse buying behaviours. At times like this, speech writing is fundamental as it helps students practise their writing skills, communicate their thoughts and feelings, and exchange ideas with their peers simultaneously. With the broad selection of online learning tools, including Google Classroom, Google Jamboard, Google Form, Google Meet, and YouTube, implementing e-portfolio is a timely and sustainable practice in online writing lessons.

Topic:	Think Before You Shop
Objectives:	*By the end of the double-lesson, the students are able to . . .*
	1 ***acquire*** knowledge about structural, stylistic, and linguistic features of a speech through authentic speeches delivered by celebrities, actors, actresses, and politicians
	2 ***produce*** a speech about impulse buying that fulfils the content, organisation, and language requirements
	3 ***correct*** common grammatical errors and ***use*** effective feedback to make text improvements collaboratively
Level:	Key stage 3 – F.3 students (Grade 9)
Duration:	2 hours (Two double lessons)
Resources:	• Emma Watson – Gender Equality
	• www.youtube.com/watch?v=nIwU-9ZTTJc
	• Steve Jobs – Stay Hungry, Stay Foolish
	• www.youtube.com/watch?v=1i9kcBHX2Nw
	• Ed Sheeran – Embrace Your Weirdness
	• https://youtu.be/kCK3cR3Pz2c
	• Elon Musk – Think Big & Dream Even Bigger
	• https://youtu.be/BDIRabVP24o
	• Barack Obama – Yes, We Can
	• www.youtube.com/watch?v=mi8N5gDVpeg&t
	• Ellen DeGeneres – Be True to Yourself
	• www.youtube.com/watch?v=bDth6cv5raI
	• Emily Blunt – Women's Education
	• https://youtu.be/ya7DNE1YZVs
	• Lady Gaga – Mental Health & Self Care
	• https://youtu.be/ZHpyfTC_Ovo

(*Continued*)

Table 6.1 (Continued)

Platform:	• Google Meet (https://meet.google.com/)
	• Google Classroom (https://classroom.google.com/)
	• Google Jamboard (https://jamboard.google.com/)
	• Google Form (https://docs.google.com/forms/)
	• YouTube (www.youtube.com)

Steps:
1   Lead-in:
1.1   Play a video of a speech delivered by Steve Jobs
1.2   Invite students to comment on the speech based on the following guiding questions:
1.2.1 Does the speaker manage to get the immediate attention of the audience?
1.2.2 Does the speaker connect well with the audience?
1.2.3 Does the speech have a clear structure?
1.2.4 Is it easy for the audience to follow?
1.2.5 Are ideas presented logically and clearly?
1.2.6 Does the speaker successfully end the speech with a call to action?
1.2.7 Does the speaker incorporate any special language features in the speech?
1.3   Discuss important structural, stylistic, and linguistic features in the speech with the class
2   While-tasks:
2.1   Tell students to get into groups of four and select a leader for each group
2.2   Invite group leaders to randomly select one of the eight great speeches chosen by the teacher
2.3   Instruct students to brainstorm ideas collaboratively by using Jamboard, an online digital interactive whiteboard developed by Google
2.4   Invite each group to share their observations with the class
2.5   Assign a writing task to students and remind them to apply the speech writing techniques they have learnt from their peers
2.5.1 You are the Head Peer Counsellor. There is a growing concern expressed by parents that students have difficulties managing their pocket money after entering secondary school. You are now writing a 250-word speech about this topic to be given at the next hall assembly, where all junior form students will attend. In your speech, talk about the following: (1) the causes of impulse buying, (2) the effects of impulse buying, and (3) advice to F.1–3 students to be aware of advertisements that are misleading.
2.6   Require students to complete a self-evaluation writing checklist before submitting their work
3   Post-tasks:
3.1   Offer writing feedback to students via a Google form
3.1.1 https://forms.gle/SSRzvLKmv13oSBnx9
3.2   Instruct students to complete the form collaboratively
3.2.1 Part A Common grammatical mistakes
3.2.2 Part B Problematic sentences

4	Consolidation:
4.1	Showcase students' outstanding work
4.2	Invite students to comment on the outstanding work with an emphasis on the structural, stylistic, and linguistic features
4.3	Ask the star writers to read a part of their speech
4.4	Show appreciation to the star writers

Additional Note (if any):
1 To facilitate the lesson flow, it is crucial to familiarise students with the wide variety of online tools and establish a day-to-day routine before integrating multiple tools into one lesson.

(The lesson plan was written by Mr Marcus Lau, an in-service English teacher in Hong Kong.)
Examples of Students' Output on Google Jamboard

Conclusion

Chapter 6 first explained the rise of digital portfolio tools. Then it presented a tripartite rationale behind e-portfolio application, including personalised, reflective, and collaborative learning. The chapter further discussed five principles, which assist teachers to select a right tool for their portfolio programmes, namely learner digital literacy, age, individual differences, purpose of instructional technology, and levels of technology integration. It went on to introduce three common digital portfolio platforms, such as blogs, customised portfolio applications, and websites, followed by a review of three popular tools which support classroom-based writing instruction in various contexts. These tools include Google Workspace for Education, ClassDojo, and FreshGrade. Although these digital tools are up to date at the time of writing, technology is changing very fast and new features, functions, and tools are being developed continuously. It is unavoidable that they may rapidly be replaced by new tools in the years to come. Chapter 6 ends with a mini-research task, which encourages readers to gain basic research insights and experience about how to utilise a suite of Google tools to broaden their writing instruction more effectively.

References

Armstrong, D., & Armstrong, G. (2022). *Educational trends exposed: How to be a critical consumer*. Routledge.

Hand, R., Bell, T. W., & Kent, D. (2012). *Mahara ePortfolios beginner's guide: Create your own ePortfolio and communities of interest within an educational and professional organization* (2nd ed.). Packt.

Johnson, L., & Kawasaki, G. (2017). *Cultivating communication in the classroom: Future-ready skills for secondary students*. Corwin.

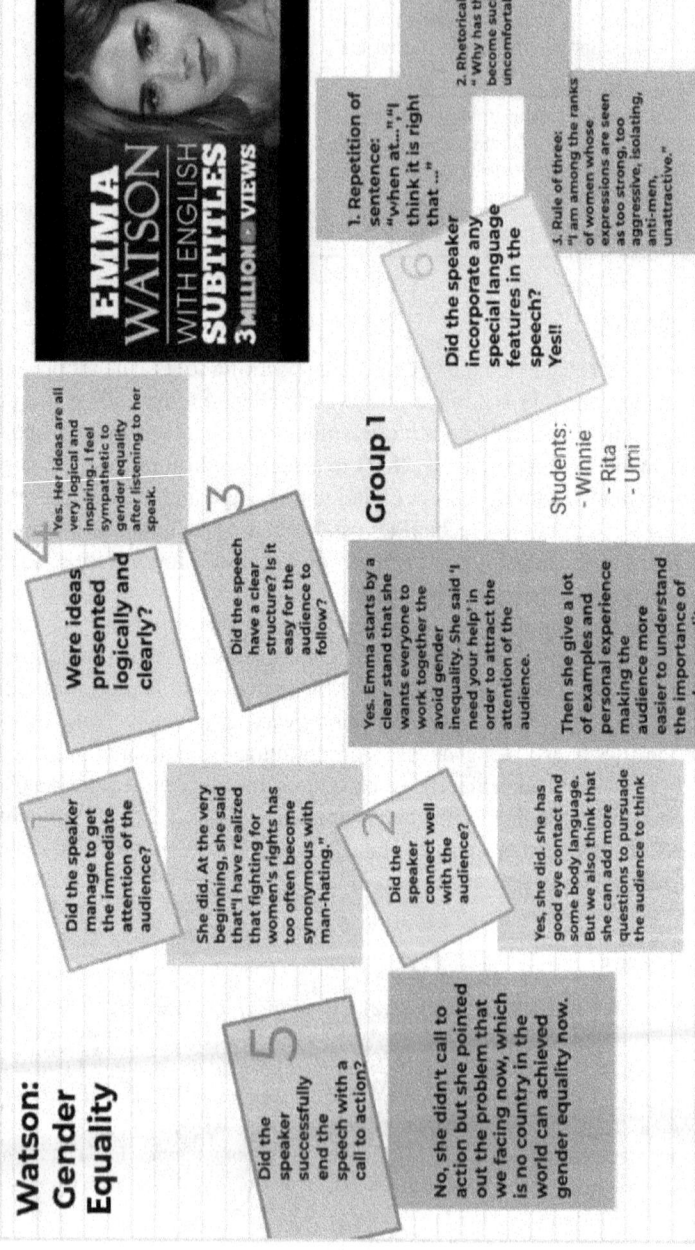

Digital Portfolio Application Tools   83

Group 3

Students:
- Darren
- Johnny
- McQueen
- Edmond

1 Did the speaker manage to get the immediate attention of the audience?

Yes. She first engages with the audience by sharing her personal motherhood which successfully got ahold of the audience's attention since these are little-known facts about Emily.

2 Did the speaker connect well with the audience?

Yes. She connected with the audience, she asked many questions and answer the questions in a humorous ways.

Emily, as one of the best actress I know, is the ablest in making all sorts of facial expressions. For example, she wore a surprised and confusing face when she touched on

3 Did the speech have a clear structure? Is it easy for the audience to follow?

Yes, her speech had a clear structure.

Yes. She first said a joke about her daughter and her to open the solemn atmosphere around the place. Those audience laughed and started to relax and listening what Emily was going to share.

4. Were ideas presented logically and clearly?

Yes, she presented her speech very well.

5. Did the speaker successfully end the speech with a call to action?

Yes, emily has successfully end the speech with a call for action. As the speech is about women's education, she lastly encouraged women over the world to change the education system so that women enjoy the same right and chance receiving an education by saying "even one woman (Malala) could make such an effort, how about 130 million women ?

This motivates women to fight for their right

6. Did the speaker incorporate any special language features in the speech?

She used a very clever comparison to appeal to her audience — "Because if one girl with an education can change the world, well we just have to imagine what 130 million can do."

By comparing Malala to a hundred million individuals. This can strongly impress the fact that everyone has a potent power to change the how the society treats women on the audience.

84 Digital Portfolio Application Tools

Group 5

Students:
Kitty
Hazel
Chloe
Hera

1 Did the speaker manage to get the immediate attention of the audience?
2 Did the speaker connect well with the audience?
3 Did the speech have a clear structure? Is it easy for the audience to follow?
4 Were ideas presented logically and clearly?
5 Did the speaker successfully end the speech with a call to action?
6 Did the speaker incorporate any special language features in the speech?

1 Yes, he did. He used the phrase "Hello, Chicago," to greet the audience (who were in Chicago back then) and keeps repeating that he would provide the answer to democracy in the U.S.

2 Yes, he did. He used using "you" and the inclusive "we" to include the audience as one of the people who are contributing to the democracy, showing he is well aware of the people he is speaking to.

3 Obama's speech did not have very refined structures. He instead used examples, for instance his personal stories during his presidential campaign, and the underprivileged as well. His speech is still easy to follow, however, because of his use of examples had a common trait among them – they are all examples of hardships, and with the use of "Yes, we can." he encourages the audience to press on despite the difficulties.

4 Yes, it is. (Refer to question 3)

5 The main message of the speech is to point out that the U.S. is suffering a lot now, a bunch of people faces various difficulties. Therefore, Obama wants everyone in the U.S. to take action because unity is the only way to let the U.S. become better and stronger nation.

Moreover, the message is clearly delivered in a clear manner which makes the whole presntation understandable and persuasive with clarity.

Each point is pointed out.

"And where we are met with cynicism and doubts and those who tell us that we can't, we will respond with that timeless creed that sums up the spirit of a people: Yes, we can."

6 Obama had emphasised that his speech would be the answer to the U.S.'s democracy, and the anaphora of "It's the answer" reinforced the point he tries to make.

Apart from that, Obama also persistently added "Yes, we can." behind every each of his points.

This lays emphasis towards how people are capable of strengthening the U.S. and enhance the welfare of the country.

Obama's speech, however, did not include a lot of questions as it is more focused on empowering the audience's spirits and also overcoming the difficulties in the nation.

Rule of three: "Block by block, brick by brick, calloused hand by calloused hand." / "There's new energy to harness, new jobs to be created, new schools to build, and threats to meet, alliances to repair."

Lam, R. (2021). Using ePortfolios to promote assessment of, for, as learning in EFL writing. *The European Journal of Applied Linguistics and TEFL, 10*(1), 101–120.

Moorhouse, B. L. (2019). Seesaw: Https://web.seesaw.me. *RELC Journal, 50*(3), 493–496.

Moorhouse, B. L., & Beaumont, A. M. (2020). Involving parents in their children's school-based English language writing using digital learning. *RELC Journal, 51*(2), 259–267. https://doi.org/10.1177/0033688219859937

Navarre, A. (2019). *Technology-enhanced teaching and learning of Chinese as a foreign language* (1st ed., Vol. 1). Routledge.

Puentedura, R. (2014). *SAMR and Bloom's taxonomy: Assembling the puzzle.* www.commonsense.org/education/articles/samr-and-blooms-taxonomy-assembling-the-puzzle

Renwick, M. (2017). *Digital portfolios in the classroom: Showcasing and assessing student work.* ASCD.

Russell, V., & Murphy-Judy, K. (2021). *Teaching language online: A guide for designing, developing, and delivering online, blended, and flipped language courses.* Routledge.

Shaban, E. A., & Abobaker, R. (2022). *Policies, practices, and protocols for the implementation of technology into language learning.* Information Science Reference, IGI Global.

Stefani, L., Mason, R., & Pegler, C. (2007). *The educational potential of e-portfolios: Supporting personal development and reflective learning.* Routledge.

Storch, N. (2019). Collaborative writing. *Language Teaching, 52*(1), 40–59.

Yancey, K. B. (2004). Postmodernism, palimpsest, and portfolios: Theoretical issues in the representation of student work. *College Composition and Communication, 55*(4), 738–761.

7 Vignette 1
Using Digital Portfolios to Facilitate Pre-School Learners' Literacy Development

Introduction

In more and more countries, English language is being taught at a younger and younger age. It is now common for students as young as three years to receive English language instruction as part of their pre-school education. Obviously, pre-school learners (defined here as children between the age of three and seven) present unique challenges for language teachers as they do not have the cognitive maturity to handle abstract language forms, nor can they be analytical about language (Ng, 2019). Furthermore, many of them may have not learned to read or write in their first languages yet and may not have a strong awareness of print conventions (Puchta & Elliott, 2017). However, as many teachers of pre-school learners will attest, they are naturally inquisitive and motivated to learn about the world and its languages (Ng, 2019). They desire the ability to understand and communicate meaning to people around them. They rely on sensory, emotional, and physical experiences to make sense of the physical and situational world they are in. However, they rely on adults to help guide them to make sense of what they are experiencing.

Therefore, language teachers need to design developmentally appropriate, immersive, fun, and meaningful activities which can help them develop their confidence, coordination, understanding of logical sequences, and thought processes (Puchta & Elliott, 2017). For literacy and writing, the primary topic of this book, pre-school learners are at the very early stage of their literacy development. Some may recognise a few letters or words but probably cannot make sense of long chains of words, nor have the fine motor skills to hold a pencil for long periods of time or form letters correctly. They may be able to copy or imitate writing, but it will not look like writing in the traditional sense.

Therefore, teachers need to create rich shared literacy experiences, which provide opportunities for students to express their thoughts and

DOI: 10.4324/9781003295860-8

ideas through dialoguing with the teacher or their peers (Slattery & Willis, 2001). Furthermore, teachers need to implement playful and fun activities that focus on developing learners' literacy skills in a balanced way. When we engage in literacy activities, such as reading, we activate two types of knowledge: what we know about meaning (top-down processing) and what we know about language (bottom-up processing) (Nuttall, 2005; Shin & Crandall, 2014). Ideally, our curriculum and instruction should help learners develop both bottom-up and top-down processing skills (Shin & Crandall, 2014).

For bottom-up processing skills, such as recognising sound-spelling relationships, teachers can get students to make letters out of modelling clay, play letter sound bingo, or sing songs that include rhythm and rhyme. For top-down skills, such as building world knowledge and genre awareness, teachers can conduct shared reading and storytelling sessions, where they read aloud a text with students joining in, using stories with repetitive patterns but rich visuals to support meaning and shared writing, where the teacher acts as a scribe and co-constructs a simple text with students contributing ideas and language (Moorhouse, 2020).

For example, to be able to successfully read a fairy-tale story, like the "Three Little Pigs", students need to have some awareness of the characteristics of wolves and pigs, that different house building materials (at least that bricks are stronger than hay!), and that stories are fictional where a problem needs to be solved. Importantly, while both reading and writing require the development of bottom-up and top-down processing skills (Nuttall, 2005; Shin & Crandall, 2014), writing provides additional demands. Writers need to be able to activate these skills, as well as physical fine motor skills, such as handwriting or typing, in the production of a text. Therefore, writing activities need to be carefully thought-out and purposeful in the pre-school classroom where writing is as much a physical task as a literacy one.

In addition, pre-school learners may not have the technological competence to use digital technologies effectively, the fine motor skills to use keyboards, nor have the awareness needed to navigate online spaces safely and securely. Therefore, teachers need to choose and use digital technologies wisely. So, given the specific characteristics of pre-school learners and their needs, how might digital portfolios help facilitate their literacy development? The following vignette presents the use of a learning management system specifically designed for young learners (Moorhouse, 2019), Seesaw (https://web.seesaw.me) and how it has been used as a digital portfolio by pre-school language teachers to their students' literacy development.

Vignette

The school

The pre-school (kindergarten) is a private kindergarten offering bilingual (Cantonese and English) classes. It is located in Kowloon, Hong Kong. It consists of four grades, Pre-nursery (2–3-year-olds), K1 (3–4-year-olds), K2 (4–5-year-olds), and K3 (5–6-year-olds). Each class consists of 20–25 students taught by two teachers – a local English teacher and a Chinese teacher. Each classroom is equipped with a suite of tablets and Wi-Fi. The kindergarten aims to create a nurturing environment that can help prepare its students for a global society. The English-language curriculum is organised into theme-based units. Themes include festivals, cultures, and customs; the environment and nature; family, and so on. Each unit has specific learning objectives related to the English language but also learners' social, emotional, and physical development. To action the objectives, teachers design various student-centred activities, including shared reading, collaborative games, singing songs and rhymes, arts and crafts, and shared writing. To connect in and out of class learning, short home-learning activities are provided that complement the in-class activities.

The digital portfolio programme

To help students showcase their language learning and literacy development, keep a record of the different activities they engage in and out of the classroom, and keep parents informed of their children's learning and development, the school decided to adopt the use of the learning management system (LMS), Seesaw as a digital portfolio. While other platforms were available (see Chapter 6 for detailed critics of different digital portfolio platforms), Seesaw was selected due to its ease of use (no e-mail or password required) and provision of a "family" version, which allows students to share their work with their family and wider community. The LMS interface can be in various different languages, meaning parents who do not speak English could still participate. A teacher can set up a Seesaw Class for a group of learners. Only students and parents invited by the teacher to view or contribute to the class can have access. Teachers have various controls which allow them to choose whether they wish to "approve" student contributions and comments or not. This means they can maintain a safe and secure online space.

Once students enter a class, they can create work directly on Seesaw in various multimodal formats, including videos, photos, texts, drawings, and hyperlinks. They can also import documents either from Google Classroom or from their device. Photos and drawings can be annotated with captions, labels, and audio-recordings. These are posted into the students' own learning journal and can be organised into folders for different activities or themes. This becomes where students can demonstrate their learning and observe their progress over time. After students have posted something, the teacher can approve it and it becomes viewable on the class journal for students and parents (if invited) to "like" or comment on. Comments can be written or voice recorded. In addition to students posting self-selected work, teachers can assign an activity for students to complete. They can create an activity themselves with audio or video instructions or examples, and templates for student responses, or they can search and select activities from a library of ready-made activities organised by grade level (e.g. Kindergarten) and subject area (e.g. English language learners).

The features of the LMS make it suitable for use as a space for compiling a digital portfolio with pre-school language learners. The following are some ways the school utilised Seesaw for bottom-up and top-down processing skills development.

Using Seesaw for bottom-up processing skills development

As stated previously, bottom-up processing skills are important to young learners' literacy development. Developing awareness of sound–spelling relationships, recognising high-frequency words, and reading and writing simple phonetically regular words, such as simple three-letter words, are important to early reading and writing. The teachers recognise this importance and have developed a number of sensory and physical in-class and out-of-class activities and games to help learners develop the skills. In the following, a number of activities used to develop and practice bottom-up literacy skills are suggested:

- Modelling clay letter making: In this activity, students make a letter out of modelling clay, take a photo of it, and upload it to their journal (see Figure 7.1). They can add a voice recording of

the letter name and sound. Magnetic letters can also be used for creating simple words.
- Photos of things that start with . . . : In this activity, students are given a letter name or sound and asked to find objects that start with that letter, take a photo of it, and upload it to their journal. They can add a voice recording of the letter name and sound and name of the object.
- Label the picture of photo: In this activity, students are given a picture or photo and letters or words. They have to move the correct letter or word next to the objects in the picture or photo and submit it to their journal. A good digital tool that teachers can use to create this activity is Wordwall. It is a web-based tool where teachers can create simple word games for students to play in and out of class.
- Sight word read aloud: In this activity, students are given a list of words, asked to audio-record them, and submit them to their journal.
- Letter, word, or sentence tracing: In this activity, students are given a letter, word, or sentence to trace using the pencil annotation tool. It is best completed on a touchscreen device such as a tablet.
- Letter art: In this activity, students make a piece of art in the shape of a letter. It is good to match the letter to a key word that it starts with (see Figure 7.2).
- Word or sentence unjumbling: In this activity, students are given a simple word (e.g. cat/dog) or sentence (e.g. I am a boy) jumbled up (e.g. tac/ boy am a I) with a picture to support meaning (see Figure 7.3). They need to reorganise the letters or words to match the picture. They can then audio-record the word or sentence and submit it to their journal.
- Teacher modelling videos: In this activity, the teacher uploads a video to Seesaw of them writing letters or words so students can see how a letter or word is written and can imitate the teacher's actions.
- Sorting sounds and words: In this activity, students are given a table with various columns headed by different sounds (e.g. p/t/s) or categories (pet/farm animals) and words to organise into the column based on their first letter sound or theme.

The teachers use a combination of these activities within a theme-based unit so as to ensure students have plenty of opportunities to

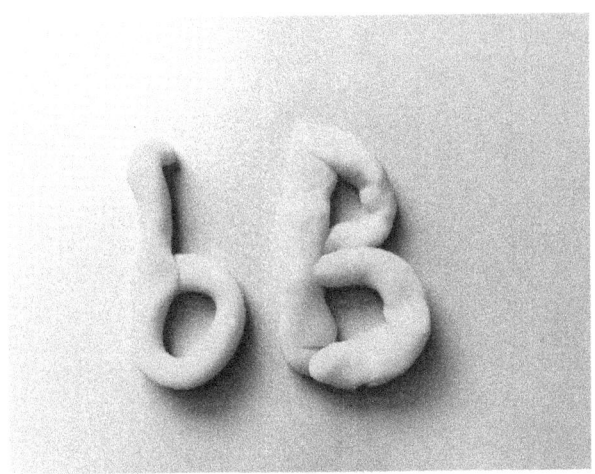

Figure 7.1 Modelling clay letter making

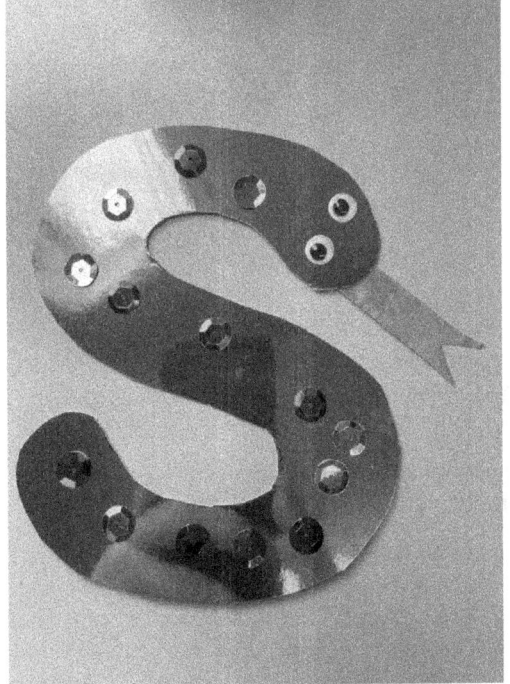

Figure 7.2 Letter art

Figure 7.3 Letter, word, or sentence jumble

develop bottom-up processing skills. Student portfolios are reviewed by teachers and shared in class to celebrate learner success and motivate them to continue practising their bottom-up skills.

Using Seesaw for top-down processing skills development

Equally important as bottom-up processing skills to early literacy development is top-down processing skills development. Top-down processing skills are concerned with the world or life knowledge and genre knowledge we bring to reading and writing (Shin & Crandall, 2014). The teachers recognise that focusing on letters, words, and sentences alone is not enough to ensure their students develop literacy skills. Therefore, they expose students to a rich literacy environment where they get to experience reading and writing through fun, scaffolded, and dialogic activities both in-class and out-of-class within their theme-based curriculum. Using Seesaw provides a number of benefits for top-down literacy skills development. First, it offers a space for teachers to disseminate materials to students for them to engage with in and out of the classroom – this could be reading texts, like stories, hyperlinks to videos on video-hosting sites (e.g. YouTube), or tailor-made videos, providing an audience and readers to students' written work, including classmates and parents, and can become a space for interaction around students' literacy work. The camera function allows teachers and students to share and archive physical work they have created into their Seesaw portfolio. The following are a number of activities used to develop and practice top-down processing skills, as well as the way Seesaw is used to facilitate, enhance, and record these activities:

- Shared reading of big books: In this activity, the teacher and students read a large version of a children's picture book together. The activity is highly dialogic with the teacher asking questions, students taking on the roles of characters, and lots of opportunities for students to share their personal feelings about the book. Teachers supplement the shared reading by recording themselves reading the book aloud and sharing it on Seesaw. This allows students to engage with the book out-of-class and even respond to it using the response options, for example "liking" the video.
- Reading response activities: In these activities, teachers develop simple activity sheets, games, or materials that relate or respond to the big books used during the shared reading. These can include sequencing scenes from the story, acting out the story using puppets or cut-outs, or drawing their favourite character or part of the story. Students or teachers can take a photo or video of their work or performance and upload it to Seesaw.
- Teacher modelling videos: In this activity, the teacher can upload to Seesaw a video of them creating a simple text, for example a personal description with a photo or drawing. Students can then watch the model and create a similar text.
- Shared writing: In this activity, the teacher and students co-construct a text together. To reduce the demands of writing, the teacher acts as the scribe and through questioning, elicits ideas

from students of what to include in the text. Teachers can create parallel stories (adapted from famous stories), or graphic organisers (e.g. mind maps/story mountains), to help organise the ideas. Teachers can take a photo of the final text and put it on Seesaw. They can read the text aloud or invite students to read the text aloud and share the audio or video-recording on Seesaw. For out-of-class learning, students can be asked to draw pictures to illustrate the story they created and add the illustrations to Seesaw.

- Responding to classmates' work: In this activity, students engage with each other's work on Seesaw and provide oral and written comments. Teachers can provide sentence stems, for example "I think your writing is". And encourage students to use "emojis" and response icons, for example "liking" to comment on their work (Wong & Moorhouse, 2018). Parents can also be encouraged to give positive comments to their children's work. Parents may also need clear instructions on how best to comment and respond to their child's work on the LMS (Moorhouse & Beaumont, 2020).
- Sharing home, school, and family life: In this activity, the teacher can ask students to take photos of different aspects of their home, school, and family life, such as events, hobbies, or likes, and share them on Seesaw. Students can be asked to provide simple captions using the annotation tool or provide a voice-over recording. This activity can be done regularly acting as a digital diary of the students' pre-school life.
- English in my community: In this activity, students can be tasked with finding examples of English in their neighbourhood and taking photos. It could be the name of shops, in magazines, or anywhere they see English. They can upload the photos to Seesaw. This activity can help learners recognise the extent of usage of English in their environment.

It is important to choose the kinds of genres young learners read and write carefully. Stories with repetitive plots and engaging illustrations are excellent resources. Teachers can also co-construct stories with their students, as these allow for lots of creativity and imagination. For personal writing though, it is best to keep activities simple and personal – short descriptions of themselves, family members, likes, and dislikes can work best. Young learners love talking about themselves and telling others about their lives. Many pre-school teachers teach a diverse group of learners. Students can have various levels of proficiency and literacy skills. If this is the case, providing learner choices of the tasks they complete, and assigning more open tasks, can help teachers cater for students' different needs and abilities.

Preparing students for the use of Seesaw

Given that the school is a pre-school, the students do not have their own digital devices and lack technological competence. Therefore, the LMS is introduced slowly to the learners with different features and functions introduced as students transition from PN to K3. In PN, primarily, the teacher takes responsibility for uploading and sharing students' work on Seesaw. They will largely take photos of their physical work and post them on the Seesaw Class. Then, in K1, students are taught how to take photos themselves using the programme and post them on the Seesaw Class. In K2, more home-based learning activities are assigned, and students are shown how to annotate images, audio voice-overs, create videos directly on Seesaw, and "like" their classmates' posts. Then, in K3, students are shown how to add written text to documents they create and provide simple written responses to their classmates' posts.

Parental involvement on Seesaw

The school recognised the important role parents play in their child's language learning and also parents' desire to know what their child is learning at school. With physical paper-based portfolios, parents may only be able to see students' schoolwork once or twice a semester. However, digital portfolios can be accessed any time. Seesaw has a family app so parents can participate in their child's Seesaw Class. The school arranges a briefing session every semester to inform parents of the use and functions of Seesaw and let them know their expectations. Parents have the opportunity to ask questions. Suggestions are provided on when and how to view, like, and comment on their child's posts on Seesaw. The teachers felt it was important to give parents a role on Seesaw, so they know how they should engage with their child's work. Parents are, therefore, asked to take up the role of "audience" and comment on their children's posts accordingly. They are given a list of sentence stems they can use to respond and encourage, such as "I really love", "I think your work is". Throughout the year, the teacher sends messages through Seesaw to update parents on what their children have been doing and invite them to participate in Seesaw. The response from parents has been encouraging and students are visibly happy when they see their parents have viewed, liked, or commented on their posts on Seesaw.

Principles of using digital portfolios with very young language learners

The vignette shows how one pre-school has utilised a digital portfolio as a tool to help them facilitate their students' literacy development while providing an opportunity for parents to become involved in their child's language learning. The teachers had to think carefully about how and why they wanted to use digital portfolios and what platforms to use that matched their needs, as well as the competence of their very young students. The following are four principles that might help guide you to develop your own digital portfolio programme in a kindergarten language classroom:

> **Principle 1: Choose an LMS carefully:** Very young language learners do not have the technological competence to use complex digital tools or platforms nor the linguistic knowledge to navigate instructions. Selecting an LMS with simple login procedures and the option for students to post photos and short videos will mean students can use the tool effectively.
>
> **Principle 2: Integrate digital portfolios into a rich and holistic student-centred literacy programme:** For digital portfolio to be a useful learning and teaching practice, it is important that the language curriculum contains activities and experiences that address both bottom-up and top-down literacy skills development.
>
> **Principle 3: Involve parents in the digital portfolio programme:** Parents can often be neglected in the language classroom. However, their involvement can increase student motivation and engagement. It is important that teachers prepare parents for their role and provide ideas for how parents can be involved in the school's digital portfolio programme.

Principle 4: Introduce digital portfolio progressively: Pre-school learners can lack some of the key knowledge and competence needed to use the digital tools required for digital portfolio. Teachers can slowly introduce different ways of using the technology over the pre-primary years. This will ensure students do not become overwhelmed and the practices can be sustainable.

Conclusion

This chapter presented the specific characteristics of pre-school learners and how we need to develop teaching activities to address them. It has shown how one school has used the digital platform Seesaw as a digital portfolio tool as a space for students to share their work and interact with one another, teachers, and parents.

It is important that at a young age, children have a positive experience of learning languages and see the process as fun and meaningful. While we may wish for them to master "the basics" like letter formation and spelling early on, there can be issues if we spend too much time on this. For example we can stifle their natural and innate interest in learning and make our and future teachers' jobs harder as we will need to re-engage our learners and motivate them to learn again. Therefore, we need to develop a balanced student-centred curriculum that helps learners see language as a tool for meaning-making and expression of ideas, thoughts, and feelings. Within our literacy teaching, digital portfolios can help. They provide a space for students to share their work and get positive feedback on their effort and performance which can motivate them to keep learning. It can also provide a long-term record of their language development over time. Teachers and parents can help students review their portfolios from time to time to show them what they have learned and how they have improved. This can increase student self-awareness and increase their learning autonomy. We encourage teachers of pre-school learners to consider ways to implement digital portfolio into their language classes.

Discussion questions

After reading the chapter, discuss and consider the following questions to help consolidate your understanding and connect what you are learning to your own classroom or future classroom.

1   What might be some of the benefits and challenges of using digital portfolios with very young language learners?
2   How might kindergarten teachers integrate digital portfolios into the language curriculum?
3   How might kindergarten teachers select a digital platform to use with their young language learners?
4   How might teachers prepare and scaffold students and parents to use the digital platform for digital portfolio?

Resources

The following is a list of useful websites and resources related to teaching language to very young learners and digital portfolios:

The British Council has a number of useful resources for teachers of very young language learners, including teaching ideas, lesson plans, and materials: Visit: www.teachingenglish.org.uk

WETA public television has developed a website called "Reading Rockets", which specifically focuses on teaching literacy to very young and young learners. The website is a good resource for information on curriculum design and instructional practices. Visit: www.readingrockets.org

Useful platforms, apps, and digital tools

The following is a list of digital tools and platforms mentioned in this chapter:

Seesaw

Seesaw is a classroom learning platform specifically designed for young learners. It has a free option and a subscription option. Its user-friendly functions and multimodal text features make it a good platform for digital portfolio pedagogies in kindergartens. There are many resources and teaching ideas available on its website. Visit Seesaw https://web.seesaw.me/lessons

YouTube

YouTube is a video-sharing site. Teachers can create and post videos to the site. The videos can be marked as unlisted, accessible only through a unique link. The teacher can provide the link on the classroom learning platform for students to access. Visit: Youtube.com

Wordwall

Wordwall is a web-based tool for creating teaching resources. It has a wide range of templates that can be used to make tailor-made digital and printable activities for students to complete. Visit: wordwall.net

References

Moorhouse, B. L. (2019). Seesaw: Https://web.seesaw.me. *RELC Journal, 50*(3), 493–496. https://doi.org/10.1177/0033688218781976

Moorhouse, B. L. (2020). *Writing with young English language learners*. RELC Portfolio Series. SEAMEO Regional Language Centre.

Moorhouse, B. L., & Beaumont, A. (2020). Involving parents in their children's school-based English language writing using digital learning. *RELC Journal*. https://doi.org/10.1177/0033688219859937

Ng, M. L. (2019). Second language literacy instruction for pre-primary learners in Hong Kong: Using stories, songs, and games. In B. L. Reynolds & M. F. Teng (Eds.), *English literacy instruction for Chinese speakers* (pp. 57–73). Singapore.

Nuttall, C. (2005). *Teaching reading skills in a foreign language* (3rd ed.). Palgrave Macmillan.

Puchta, H., & Elliott, K. (2017). *Activities for very young learners*. Cambridge University Press.

Shin, J. K., & Crandall, J. (2014). *Teaching young learners English*. National Geographic Learning.

Slattery, M., & Willis, J. (2001). *English for primary teachers: A handbook of activities and classroom language* (Vol. 1). Oxford University Press.

Wong, K. M., & Moorhouse, B. L. (2018). Writing for an audience: Inciting creativity among young English language bloggers through scaffolded comments. *TESOL Journal, 9*(4). https://doi.org/10.1002/tesj.389

8 Vignette 2
Adopting Digital Portfolios to Promote Primary School Learners' Self-Regulated Learning in Writing

Introduction

It is common in most countries and regions for students to start learning English in primary schools. In some contexts, typically those with British colonial histories, it is a core school subject as it is still widely used in government bureaus and higher education. In others, English is taught to give students a "head start" in this increasingly important lingua franca of international business and trade.

A challenge when conceptualising effective language teaching methodologies in the primary school years is the range in ages, with younger learners and older learners having very different needs and abilities (Pinter, 2017). For example when teaching a six-year-old English for the first time, we may focus on oral language predominately, as they will still be learning the concepts of print in their first language. Whereas a ten-year-old will likely have a good command of literacy skills in their first language, using written language may support them in their process of acquiring English. Therefore, our curriculum designs and classroom methodology need to reflect the linguistic, cognitive, affective, and social development of our learners as they progress through the primary years – and at the same time, recognising that all learners are unique and develop at different speeds (Pinter, 2017).

We do know that by creating certain conditions in the language classroom, we are more likely to have successful teaching and subsequently language learning (Read, 2015). First, we need to create a safe, supportive, and holistic learning environment. Second, we need to develop student-centred experiences where learners can set goals, make decisions, and take ownership over their language learning. Third, we need to provide rich exposure to language, with ample opportunities for natural interaction and meaningful

DOI: 10.4324/9781003295860-9

repetition. Fourth, we need to design and implement activities and tasks that give learners the chance to use language in creative ways, engaging in dramas, storytelling, and writing.

The focus of this book is specifically to the sub-skill of writing. Many primary school language teachers will attest that writing seems to be the most difficult of the four skills to teach and for students to master. Indeed, to become successful writers, young learners need to have the following knowledge, skills, and attitude (Moorhouse, 2020, p. 4): (1) language knowledge – learners need knowledge of the mechanics of English, for example writing conventions; (2) genre knowledge – learners need knowledge of a variety of genres, for example stories, recipes, recounts; (3) content knowledge: learners need knowledge of the topic they are writing about, for example animals, food, heroes; (4) writing skills –learners need the skills to develop and shape a piece of writing; and (5) a positive attitude –learners need to be self-directed, self-aware, open-minded, confident, and motivated to write. As writing is a social act, learners need to be able to use language to express meanings to their audience (Cameron, 2001; Ryan, 2014). For example if students are tasked with writing a letter, they need to understand the social purpose of a letter – to correspond a message across physical distance, they need to have a receiver in mind, they need a reason to write to them (and why writing a letter is the best way to communicate the message), they need to know the structure and organisation of a letter, they need knowledge of the topic of the letter, and they need to have the language knowledge needed to construct the words, sentences, and paragraphs to write the letter. Also, they need the motivation and interest to write the letter. If any of these things are missing, then it is likely the writing task will be unsuccessful.

Digital portfolios can be a useful tool in helping primary school students develop the knowledge, skills, and attitude needed to be successful writers mentioned earlier. Specifically, digital portfolios can be used to promote self-regulated learning. Students can regulate their learning by using metacognitive strategies, including goal-setting, reviewing, adjusting, revising, and reflecting to identify areas of strength and improvement and close the gaps between desired and current levels of knowledge and performance (Andrade & Brookhart, 2016; Lam, 2019) (see Chapter 5 for a discussion of the idea of self-regulated learning and how it relates to digital portfolios with e-feedback). Utilising digital portfolios in combination with formative feedback practices can help facilitate students' regulation of their cognition, motivation, and actions (Becker, 2015;

Hawe & Dixon, 2017), which are needed if students are to become successful writers.

So, how might a school-based digital portfolio programme capitalising on the promotion of self-regulated learning help primary school language learners develop the knowledge, skills, and attitude required to be successful writers? The following vignette introduces the curriculum design and instructional approaches of one primary school that has developed a school-based portfolio programme.

Vignette

The school

The school is a Chinese-medium government-subsidised primary school located on Hong Kong Island. It consists of six grades, Primary One (6–7-year-olds) to Primary Six (11-to-12-year-olds). Each class consists of 24–28 students of mixed English-language proficiency. The teachers are subject specialists, with each subject taught by a different teacher. Students receive eight 40-minute periods of English language lessons per week taught by an English language teacher. The school has Wi-Fi access and has initiated a bring-your-own-device scheme (BYOD) where students are required to purchase a tablet for school use. The school has a means-tested scholarship available for students who need support in purchasing a tablet.

The school-based English-language writing curriculum

As part of the school-based English-language curriculum, a process writing approach programme for the older learners in Primary Three to Six, have been initiated. The Primary One and Two writing curriculum focuses on rich language input and short personalised writing tasks. This vignette focuses on the process writing approach programme. The programme is progressive and spiralling with writing tasks designed to build on and consolidate previous tasks. Two 40-minute periods a week are dedicated to the programme with each writing task typically lasting four to five weeks to complete.

The process writing approach programme adopted by the school (see Moorhouse, 2020, for a detailed introduction to the use of the process writing approach with young learners), includes six stages: prewriting; generating and organising ideas; drafting; revising; editing; and publishing.

In the pre-writing stage, the teacher and learners discuss the purpose (why they are writing) and audience (who they are writing to), content (what they are writing about) and genre (what kind of text they are going to write) of the writing task. The teachers organise some activities to help learners build their content and genre knowledge. Teachers might engage in shared reading where they read a book with the students that includes content that could be used in their students' writing. They can help students notice and select information that they can use in their writing. This information could be organised into mind maps or graphic organisers. Sometimes, teachers initiate shared events, for example parties, or experiences, for example sports day, school picnic, for students to write about. Also, they can model and guide students to engage in independent research in the school or local library or on the Internet.

In the generating and organising ideas stage, the teacher and students think about what they are going to write. Teachers can use storybooks, photographs, short videos, shared experience, letters, or other artefacts to stimulate thinking and generate ideas. Graphic organisers can be used to help learners organise their ideas. Modelling is important at this stage, with teachers showing learners how they generate and organise their own ideas for writing. In this stage, students are moreover encouraged to set their own learning goals. These can focus on the different knowledge, skills, and attitudes required for successful writers. A task- and genre-specific rubric is provided so students know the expectations of the writing task.

In the drafting stage, students organise and structure their ideas into a first draft of a complete text. A writing frame is provided with the text structure, prompts, and questions included to help guide students. Modelling is also important at this stage. Teachers engage in shared writing with the class where they construct a text with the whole class so that students can observe and participate in the process of text construction.

In the revising stage, the aim is to improve the content and quality of the text. Teachers write questions and ideas on the students' drafts to prompt them to think of ways to improve it. They teach "mini-lessons", where they focus on a specific feature of the genre for students to include, for example using reported speech in a story. Teachers can conference with students – engaging in a one-on-one discussion about the students' drafts. They also promote buddy sharing where students read each other's drafts and give feedback.

In the editing stage, the attention turns to the language accuracy of the students' drafts. Here, teachers help guide students to correct their work. They use a combination of self-checking – encouraging students to read their own work; peer checking – ask students to read each other's work and identify language mistakes; and teacher checking – where teachers provide written corrective feedback.

In the publishing stage, students write their final draft and share it with their audience. Teachers can provide templates that mimic real-world genres, such as books, posters, and letters. Students can share their work in class, through gallery walks, read-alouds, and class conferences, or digitally, on a class blog. The teachers ensure there are opportunities for students to receive feedback from their classmates. They teach students how to give positive comments. In the early years, they provide sentence stems to scaffold comments, for example "I think your story is_____". Then, in the later years, they give a structure for students to follow, for example share your feelings about the writing, give an example of something you like, be specific about what the writer did well (Wong & Moorhouse, 2018). In this stage, students are also encouraged to reflect on their effort, performance, and learning over the whole writing process and evaluate themselves against their original goals. Teachers use the rubric introduced earlier in the process to provide feedback on the final published draft.

Throughout the four years of the programme, students engage in writing a variety of texts, including recounts, personal introductions, stories, biographies, information reports, letters, and instructional texts.

The digital portfolio programme

Initially, the school used a physical paper-based portfolio where students would archive their work as they moved through the stages of the writing process. However, with the initiation of the BYOD scheme, the teachers saw additional advantages of using a digital portfolio. Digital portfolios were chosen as they provide a space for students to record the purpose of learning, process of learning, product of learning, and reflection on learning. Also, they made it easier for students to share their work with peers and families. This makes them a good tool for promoting self-regulated learning in writing and aids the development of the knowledge, skills, and attributes needed to be a successful writer.

The English language teachers chose the Learning Management System (LMS), Google Classroom as the classroom learning platform and for the digital portfolio. While other platforms were available (see Chapter 6 for a detailed criticism of different digital portfolio platforms), Google Classroom was chosen as it is free to use and was adopted by teachers in other subjects; therefore, students and parents were familiar with its interface and functions. It is also a good central place to record all learning, not just writing. Teachers can create an assignment each time students are expected to upload something to their portfolio. Templates, including goal-setting sheets, graphic organisers, presentation slides, and checklists can be easily created, shared, and completed by students on the platform. Teachers can see who has completed the portfolio task and give feedback directly through Google Classroom. Other Google Workspace tools, such as Jamboard (a digital interactive whiteboard) and Google Slides (a presentation software), can be used for collaborative activities – such as generating ideas and sharing the outcomes of independent, group, or class research. An added advantage of Google Classroom is that any documents created will be saved in the students' own Google Drive folder. This means that as students move along their educational journey, they have a record of their previous work.

Teachers also create a class blog on Blogger as a space for students to share their final published work with parents and the wider school community.

Strategies to develop self-regulated learning

When developing the writing programme, teachers wanted students to have ownership of their learning process and product and develop students' self-regulated learning skills; namely goal-setting, reviewing, adjusting, revising, and reflecting. These activities are integrated into the aforementioned process writing approach – which aligns well with self-regulated learning principles. The following are some ways the English-language teachers utilise digital portfolios to promote self-regulated learning sub-skills in their school-based writing programme:

Content	
Before	After
I want to ... ☐ write 60 words or more ☐ use more adjectives ☐ use "talking sentences" ☐ create interesting characters ☐ include an exciting problem	I ... ☐ wrote 60 words or more ☐ used more adjectives ☐ used "talking sentences" ☐ created interesting characters ☐ included an exciting problem
Language and Organisation	
Before	After
I want to ... ☐ spell words correctly ☐ use full stops correctly ☐ use past tense correctly ☐ use speech marks correctly ☐ write in paragraphs	I ... ☐ spelt words correctly ☐ used full stops correctly ☐ used past tense correctly ☐ used speech marks correctly ☐ wrote in paragraphs
Reflections	
How do you feel about your fairy-tale story? Did you improve? What will you do next time?	

Figure 8.1 Goal-setting Sheet

Goal-setting:

- Goal-setting sheets: During the generating and organising ideas stage, teachers can guide students to set goals for their writing tasks. These goals should relate to their previous writing performance and be adjusted from task to task. A sheet with specific goals can be developed and assigned to students through Google Classroom (see Figure 8.1). They can complete it on Google Docs and submit to the teacher. The teacher and students can easily refer to their goals as they progress through the writing process. They can access their progress towards their goals at the end of the process.
- Task and genre-specific rubrics: To help students understand the writing task requirements and monitor their performance, teachers develop and provide task and genre-specific rubrics

(see Figure 8.2). These can be uploaded to the Google Classroom as a reference material for students to refer to while they are engaging in the writing process. The teachers use the same rubric for peer, self, and teacher assessment. This helps learners know their areas of strengths and improvement in each writing task.

Content

	☺	☺☺	☺☺☺
Setting and build-up	It has only two of the "who, when, where, what".	It has "who, when, where, what".	It has "who, when, where, what" and is engaging.
Problem	It has a simple problem.	It has an interesting problem.	It has an interesting and creative problem.
Resolution and Ending	It has a simple resolution and ending.	It has an interesting resolution and ending.	It has an interesting and creative resolution and ending.

Target Content Feature

	☺	☺☺	☺☺☺
Talking sentences + saying words	It has one talking sentence.	It has two or three talking sentences.	It has "who, when, where, what" and is engaging.

Language

	☺	☺☺	☺☺☺
Spelling	There are many spelling mistakes.	There are a few spelling mistakes.	There are no spelling mistakes.
Grammar	There are many grammar mistakes.	There are a few grammar mistakes.	There are no grammar mistakes.

Comments:

Figure 8.2 Sample Rubric for Fairy-Tale Stories:

Reviewing:

- Online dictionaries and writing tools: Teachers introduce different online dictionaries and writing support tools to students to use, such as WordHippo and Google Translate. Students are shown the features, and teachers discuss the benefits and limitations of the tools. Hyperlinks to the tools are provided in the class's Google Classroom for students to self-access when they think they need the tools.
- Online Word Processing: Complementary to Google Classroom is Google Docs. Google Docs is an online word processing tool. Students can create their drafts directly on Google Docs and use various features to edit and revise their drafts. Teachers can introduce various features of Google Docs to the students, so they can create more professional looking output. Teachers give written feedback directly onto students' work with the "comment" and "suggestion" functions. Files can be easily labelled to keep a record of the drafts and development of the writing piece.

Adjusting:

- Independent and collaborative content research: During the pre-writing stage, students are encouraged to engage in independent and collaborative research about the topic they will be writing about. For example if they are writing about world festivals, they could visit different websites, read books, or talk to people about festivals they celebrate or like. They can share what they find out on a collaborative space, such as Jamboard or the teacher can provide a graphic organiser template for students to complete and upload to their portfolio. This allows students to refer to the graphic organiser when they are writing their drafts.
- Genre analysis activities: During the pre-writing stage, teachers can create activities to raise students' genre knowledge. For example teachers can give students two texts, one with correct language features and one without something missing or wrong. Students can be tasked with comparing them, identifying the correct text, and discussing the reasons for their choice (see Fig. 8.3). This can help them notice the features, content, and organisation of the genre and the relationship between its features, audience, and social purpose. After the activity, students can upload the texts to their portfolio. The correct text can act as a model during their drafting.

Circle the differences. Which is the correct text? How do you know?
What does the activity tell you about the role of quantifiers in recipes?

Recipe A Grilled Tuna Melt  Makes 4 sandwiches Time: 10 minutes **Ingredients** 8 slices of bread 1 small tin of tuna 1 tablespoon of mayonnaise 8 slices of cheese **Steps** 1. Mix the tuna and mayonnaise together. 2. Put one slice of bread on a plate. 3. Put a tablespoon of the mixture on the bread, then add one slice of cheese on top. 4. Put one slice of bread on top. 5. Heat a frying pan over a medium heat. 6. When the pan is hot, put the sandwich in the frying pan. 7. Cook each sandwich for 2–3 minutes on each side or until toasted.	Recipe B Grilled Tuna Melt  Makes 4 sandwiches Time: 10 minutes **Ingredients** Some bread Some tuna Some mayonnaise Some cheese **Steps** 1. Mix the tuna and mayonnaise together. 2. Put some bread on a plate. 3. Put some of the mixture on the bread, then add some cheese on top. 4. Put some bread on top. 5. Heat a frying pan over a medium heat. 6. When the pan is hot, put the sandwich in the frying pan. 7. Cook each sandwich for 2–3 minutes on each side or until toasted.

Figure 8.3 Example Genre Analysis Activity

Revising:

- Teacher modelling videos: To provide examples of the process of writing, and not just the product, teachers can create short videos of them engaging in various aspects of the writing process. These can be posted on Google Classroom for students to access if they need support.
- Teacher mini-lessons: Teachers create a short video introducing or reminding students of a language or genre feature that they can use to enhance and improve their writing. This can be uploaded to Google Classroom for out-of-class viewing before a lesson where the students revise their work. This is a simple way to introduce the flipped classroom approach to primary school language learners. The videos should be very short and focused on one suggestion or ideas.

Reflecting:

- Self-assessment, reflection, and forward planning: During and at the end of the writing process, students can be asked to assess and reflect on their expectations, effort, performance, and learning.
- A class blog: As Google Classroom is a closed space only accessible by teachers and their students, the teachers create class blogs on Blogger as a space for students to share their work with their peers, school community, and parents. Here, students can upload their final draft for sharing with a wider audience. This allows them to celebrate their writing and feel like published authors.
- Scaffolded comments and responses: Using the Blogger "comment" function, students can be encouraged to provide positive comments to their classmates' writing and even respond to comments they receive. Students can be scaffolded to construct comments and responses. It is important that students respond as the audience.

Although many of these activities can be done without the need for a digital portfolio, the teachers attest that the portfolio acts as a space where students can see their performance grow over a period of learning. At the beginning and end of the year, teachers take time to review the students' digital portfolio entries with them. Many times, the students are shocked by how much their writing quantity and quality have improved. This motivates them to continue learning and contributing to their portfolio.

Preparing students for using digital portfolio in the primary school

As with the writing programme, which is developmental, so is the use of the digital portfolio and self-regulated learning activities. For example in Primary Three, most writing tasks are completed with pencil and paper, with students taking photos of their work and uploading it to their portfolio. However, as they progress through the years, more tasks are conducted on the LMS and digital tools, such as Google Docs. Similarly, goal-setting sheets start with a few choices for students to select from, but develop into more open, student-oriented sheets with prompts and guiding questions. For technology skills, features of the LMS used can be slowly introduced and reused throughout the primary years. It is important that an LMS with user-friendly features is chosen – this will ensure students will not need too much initial training to get started. This allows teachers to scaffold the introduction of digital portfolios and make sure students feel comfortable with their use in their language learning.

Principles of using digital portfolios with primary school language learners

The vignette shows how one primary school has used a digital portfolio programme, within their school-based writing programme, as a tool to help learners develop self-regulation over their writing development. By integrating several strategies into the programme, teachers provided ways for students to set goals, monitor their progress and performance, and evaluate their strengths and areas in need of improvement. The strategies also allow teachers to monitor students' progress and performance and provide feedback that can help learners develop their writing knowledge and skills. The following are some principles that might help guide you to develop your own digital portfolio programme in a primary school language classroom:

> **Principle 1: Align digital portfolio practices with appropriate writing teaching pedagogies:** Digital portfolios can be used as a tool to support the writing process as well as showcase the writing product. It is important that teachers consider the role of the portfolio and align it with their teaching practices accordingly.
>
> **Principle 2: Utilise appropriate digital tools to fulfil the purpose of respective activities:** Every digital tool has both affordances and constraints. It is important to select tools that help teachers and learners mediate a specific activity. For example Jamboard is a good tool for collaborative idea generating while Blogger is a good tool for publishing and sharing of final drafts of students' work.
>
> **Principle 3: Provide scaffolding to support student interaction:** Students can often struggle to comment and respond to their peer's written work. It is important to give students' specific roles, for example assistant or audience, and teach them how to respond accordingly. Teachers can spend some time in lesson, generating ideas for ways to comment on students' work.

Principle 4: Review the digital portfolios with students regularly: To help learners observe and reflect on their writing effort and performance, it is important for teachers to review the portfolio with students. In this way, they can see their development and improvement over time.

Conclusion

This chapter presented important consideration and challenges of teaching writing to primary school-age English language learners and how, through the use of a systematic school-based writing curriculum which integrates a process-genre approach to writing instruction and digital portfolio, students can develop the knowledge, skills, and attitude required to be successful writers.

It is important to remember that writing is a complex skill and takes time for students to master. As we come across new genres, for new audiences, about new topics, we can often lack the knowledge and skills we need to construct a meaningful and accurate text. We need to make our students aware of this complexity and help them become self-regulated learners, so when they come across challenges, they have ways to overcome them. Teaching activities and scaffolding are not to just help our students successfully complete the specific writing task they are doing at that time but help them improve their knowledge, skills, and attitude so they can become more successful writers in the future. Utilising digital portfolios and associated teaching approaches is one way we can help our learners achieve this aim.

Discussion questions

After reading the chapter, discuss and consider the following questions to help consolidate your understanding and connect what you are learning to your own classroom or future classroom.

1. Why are teaching and learning writing considered the hardest of the four language skills?
2. How can digital portfolios play a role in promoting self-regulated learning in the primary language classroom?
3. What challenges might teachers face when using digital portfolios with primary school-age language learners?
4. What strategies mentioned in the vignette would you consider using in your own writing lessons?
5. How might you set up a school-based digital portfolio programme in your class or school for the first time?

Resources

The following are some useful websites and resources related to teaching language to primary school learners and digital portfolios:

European Language Portfolio (ELP)

To promote learner autonomy, plurilingualism, and intercultural awareness and competence and allow users to record their language-learning achievements and their experience of learning and using languages, the Language Policy Programme of the Council of Europe developed the European Language Portfolio (ELP). The ELP website provides resources, models, and templates that can help teachers develop and implement portfolio pedagogies in their practices. Visit: www.coe.int/en/web/portfolio

Readwritethink

Readwritethink is a teaching and learning community for English language arts teachers from K-12. It has a huge range of resources, including lesson plans, templates, writing samples, and teaching ideas. There are useful ideas of how to create an online community through digital portfolios and graphic organisers for various kinds of writing genres. Most of the resources are free to download. Visit: Readwritethink.org

Sparklebox.com

Sparklebox is an online repository of teaching and learning materials. It has a vast collection of thematic materials, including model texts, templates, rubrics, and graphic organisers. Sparklebox is a subscription service. Visit: www.sparklebox.co.uk

Useful digital tools and platforms

The following is a list of digital tools and platforms mentioned in this chapter:

Jamboard

Jamboard is a collaborative whiteboard tool developed by Google. Teachers can easily create a Jamboard and invite students to collaborate on it. They can add text, images, videos, and other files. Visit: https://jamboard.google.com

Google Classroom

Google Classroom is a free classroom learning platform. Teachers can create a class for their students. They can set assignments and create spaces for students to upload and post their work. Visit: https://edu.google.com/workspace-for-education/classroom/

Blogger

Blogger is a web-based blog platform developed by Google. Teachers can create a class blog where students' work can be uploaded and commented on. The blog can be closed or open depending on the audience of the blog. Visit: blogger.com

WordHippo

WordHippo is an online thesaurus and word tool. Students can look up various word associations, including synonyms, antonyms, definitions, and pronunciations. Visit: wordhippo.com

References

Andrade, H., & Brookhart, S. M. (2016). The role of classroom assessment in supporting self-regulated learning. In D. Laveault & L. Allal (Eds.), *Assessment for learning: Meeting the challenge of implementation* (pp. 293–309). Springer.

Becker, C. (2015). Assessment and portfolios. In J. Bland (Ed.), *Teaching English to young learners: Critical issues in language teaching with 3–12 year olds*. Bloomsbury.

Cameron, L. (2001). *Teaching language to young learners*. Cambridge University Press.

Hawe, E., & Dixon, H. (2017). Assessment for learning: A catalyst for student self-regulation. *Assessment & Evaluation in Higher Education*, *42*(8), 1181–1192.

Lam, R. (2019). *Using portfolios in language teaching*. RELC Portfolio Series. SEAMEO Regional Language Centre.

Moorhouse, B. L. (2020). *Writing with young English language learners*. RELC Portfolio Series. SEAMEO Regional Language Centre.

Pinter, A. (2017). *Teaching young language learners* (2nd ed.). Oxford University Press.

Read, C. (2015). Forward. In J. Bland (Ed.), *Teaching English to young learners: Critical issues in language teaching with 3–12 year olds*. Bloomsbury.

Ryan, M. (2014). Writers as performers: Developing reflexive and creative writing identities. *English Teaching: Practice and Critique, 13*(1), 130–148.

Wong, K. M., & Moorhouse, B. L. (2018). Writing for an audience: Inciting creativity among young English language bloggers through scaffolded comments. *TESOL Journal, 9*(4). https://doi.org/10.1002/tesj.389

9 Vignette 3
Blending Assessment and Learning of Writing in the Secondary School Language Classroom via Digital Portfolios

Introduction

In nearly every country, secondary school students (usually aged between 11 and 18) are learning at least one second or foreign language. English is the most common language students will be learning. While secondary school-age language learners are still developing their literacy skills in their first language, it is likely that they have a command of "the basics" and can effectively read and write a variety of different genres. They are more cognitively and socially developed than younger learners and have started to develop metacognitive skills and affective regulation. However, depending on their previous learning experiences, interests, abilities, family background, and motivation, they can have varying degrees of second or foreign language proficiencies. Also, they are more self-conscious and self-aware of their language proficiency (Ryan & Patrick, 2001). Furthermore, in many contexts, secondary school classes can be large, with 25–45 students in one class. While students might be grouped into classes by their language proficiency, there can still be a large range of proficiencies in one class.

The large multi-levelled classroom, where students are more self-conscious and self-aware brings a variety of challenges for language teachers (Hess, 2001). First, a major challenge is developing curricula, materials, activities, and instructional approaches that can successfully cater for diverse interests, needs, proficiencies, and learning preferences. A second challenge is the amount of written work students produce. In Hong Kong, secondary school teachers often complain about the huge workload. Teachers can spend hours and hours on marking and providing feedback to student compositions. A third challenge is the increasing importance of assessments and examinations, with the end of secondary education signified by high-stakes public examinations which can determine students' future prospects. With English increasingly becoming the global language of higher education, the

DOI: 10.4324/9781003295860-10

capital that a good command of English language affords secondary school learners can be profound (Costley, 2018).

On the plus side, as secondary school language learners are more cognitively and socially developed than young learners and have begun to develop metacognition skills and affective regulation, they can engage in more complex activities and tasks (Tragant & Victori, 2006). Also, they have more knowledge of the world and technological competence which can aid their language learning. In most contexts, secondary school-age learners will feel comfortable using technology to complete various real-world tasks, such as searching for information, interacting on social media, and using various digital tools for leisure, learning, and out-of-class learning. However, they may still be developing the skills needed to critically evaluate what they read and engage with online, and their understanding of privacy, safety, ethical use of materials, and managing their identity online may be underdeveloped.

Clearly, bringing "the digital" into the language classroom helps motivate learners. English is the dominate language of the Internet and online gaming – and a resource that can help people communicate with people from different countries and contexts. Projects such as Europe's Erasmus+ eTwinning initiative www.etwinning.net/en/pub/index.htm) are specifically designed to connect students in different counties together through technology. In addition, the Internet and digital tools can help cater for learners with diverse needs and interests. There are sites about everything and tools to help with different needs (Stickler, 2022). For example if they want to learn about animals or famous places, they can visit natgeokids.com. Or if they do not know a specific word in their target language, they can use a machine translation tool such as Google Translate. With resources and tools at students' fingertips, teachers can become facilitators, helping their learners navigate the online world and guiding them to use specific tools that can help move forward their language learning.

However, the teacher's role becomes more complicated in the contexts of high-stakes public assessments. Teachers and students can worry about students' performance and often their focus shifts from enjoyment to results and outcomes (Costley, 2018), and this can lead teachers to "play it safe" and use "tried and tested" teacher-oriented instructional approaches. In Hong Kong, it is common for students, particularly in senior grades, to spend a large amount of time completing past-papers which are submitted to teachers for written corrective feedback. In such contexts, we need to find ways to satisfy the concerns of teachers, students, and parents while introducing pedagogical approaches that better utilise technology for the benefit of student learning.

Digital portfolios potentially provide a way to help connect the benefits of technology in teaching and learning of writing, with the demands of high-stakes writing assessments and examinations in the secondary school language classroom (see Chapter 4 for a detailed discussion of the use of digital portfolio for assessment). First, digital portfolios can be a space to archive and record student performance on mock examinations and tests over a period of learning. Students can observe their performance over time and analyse, with the teacher's guidance, specific tasks or questions they need to work on. If teachers combine the portfolio with online quiz platforms (e.g. Quizizz), students can get instant corrective feedback. The platforms provide important performance analytics that can help them give more targeted feedback and instruction. Second, teachers can create an online text bank of past-papers and mock papers for students to access and complete in their own time. Third, assessment criteria and rubrics can be uploaded to the digital portfolio platform for self, peer, and teacher feedback. Students' written texts, and even audio-recorded texts can be annotated by teachers – providing in-text comments that can focus students' attention on ways their work can be improved. Fourth, digital portfolios are a useful reference for students to refer to when studying or revising for assessments. Over time, teachers and students can add useful learning materials, links to digital tools and resources, exemplars, and examination tips that can aid students' examination preparation. Finally, the process of building and maintaining a digital portfolio can develop students' metacognitive skills (Becker, 2015; Hawe & Dixon, 2017), which can improve their test-taking abilities.

However, in reality, teachers can find it hard to link language teaching and high-stakes public assessments together. Often, language teaching takes a back seat to assessments preparation when the public assessments are approaching. So how might teachers blend assessment and learning of writing through the use of digital portfolio? The vignette that follows presents the case of a secondary school where the teachers implemented a digital portfolio programme to help students prepare for the public assessments.

Vignette

The school

The school is a Chinese-medium government-subsidised school located in the New Territories. It consists of six forms, Secondary One (12–13-year-olds) to Secondary Six (17–18-year-olds). There are 30 classes in the school with 34 students in each class. The teachers are subject specialists, with each subject taught by a different teacher. Students receive English lessons daily. The classes include students with mixed English language proficiencies. The classrooms are equipped with Wi-Fi access, teacher's computer, and class project. The school has initiated a bring-your-own-device scheme (BYOD), where students are required to purchase a tablet for school use.

Aligning the school-based English-language writing assessments and public assessments

In Hong Kong secondary schools, there are two main public assessments: *Territory-wide System Assessment (TSA) for English Language* and *Hong Kong Diploma of Secondary Education (HKDSE) Examinations for English Language and Literature in English* (English Language Curriculum Guide, 2017). The TSA is taken by Secondary Three students. It is designed to facilitate assessment for learning by providing schools with objective data on students' overall performance in the English language. Schools receive a report on their students' strengths and weaknesses against specific basic competencies. No information is provided on individual student performance with the data aggregated. The HKDSE is taken at the completion of the students' secondary education. Its aim is to measure students' level of attainment in the English language and literature. The writing component of the HKDSE English language assessment is weighted at 25% of the assessment. The writing component aims to assess the ability of candidates to (Hong Kong Examinations and Assessment Authority, 2022):

- write texts for different contexts, audiences, and purposes with relevant content and adequate supporting details;
- convey meaning using varied vocabulary, linguistic devices, and language patterns appropriately and accurately;
- plan and produce coherent and structured texts with ideas effectively presented and developed;
- write texts using appropriate tone, style, and register and the salient features of different genres; and
- draft and revise written texts.

To help prepare students for the public assessments, the Hong Kong Education Bureau encourages English language teachers to develop students' understanding of the learning outcomes and assessment requirements of the public assessments. To do this, they suggest "schools to provide students with tasks which reflect the learning outcomes and assessment requirements of public assessments, and are pitched at a level of difficulty appropriate to students' ability" (English Language Curriculum Guide, 2017, p. 95). Various digital resources and materials are provided to help teachers. The learning progression framework (LPF) provides a common scale and language for teachers to describe students' performance and progress in English language learning. It is divided into the four skills, listening, speaking, reading, and writing. The writing skills framework has learning outcomes pertaining to content, organisation, language, and style. They are divided into eight progressive attainment milestones. The Education Bureau website provides exemplars of students' work at each attainment level. The Student Assessment Repository (STAR) platform provides a range of assessment items and online assessment data, such as reports and qualitative descriptions about students' performance to help schools understand students' attainment and plan remediation and progression (https://star.hkedcity.net/en). It has a digital archive of more than 59,000 assessment items.

These resources and materials provide concrete descriptions of students' attainment and useful statistical data, enabling teachers to guide students to understand and monitor their own learning performance, identify areas of strengths and weaknesses, and draw up plans for progressing to the next level of achievement. They have helped the case study school develop a set of school-based writing criteria that helps students understand their performance in their school-based writing tasks and assessments. This allows students to engage in goal-setting, as they know what area they need to improve, progress monitoring, as well as self-reflection. In addition, they provide useful information to parents. Parents know how their children are progressing, what their strengths and weaknesses are, and where help might be necessary.

The digital portfolio programme

The school adopted Canvas as a learning management system (LMS). Canvas was chosen for a number of reasons. It provides an easy-to-use interface and one single login. Therefore, students do not need to remember multiple passwords. It allows for integration of other digital tools the teachers use, for example Nearpod. This means all the teaching and learning materials and resources can be found in one place. For assessments, it allows teachers to upload rubrics for specific tasks and assessments. Students can refer to these when completing tasks, and teachers can grade students' performance in the tasks. Teachers can provide written feedback or record video feedback. It has built-in analytics tools so students and learners can monitor performance and progress. Furthermore, it allows for asynchronous and synchronous communication between users, providing a space for question raising, dialogue, and collaboration around a task. When students graduate from secondary school, they can download their digital portfolio as a zip file for long-term retention.

The English language teachers use Canvas in most writing lessons. For example they regularly upload short teaching videos introducing a genre feature highlighting common mistakes or suggesting specific writing skill to students before writing lessons. They share and present their interactive presentations using Nearpod. They post the assignment criteria and task requirements and set up a submission link for students to upload their drafts. They provide feedback to students' drafts and final writing directly on Canvas. The following is an example of how the secondary school teachers use a digital portfolio in their writing lessons to prepare students for public assessments is provided.

An example writing task

The writing task comes from the Secondary Three English language programme. It is designed to help prepare students for the TSA. A past TSA writing task is used as the catalyst for the writing task (see Figure 9.1 for the writing task). Adopting genre-based approaches (see Chapter 3 for details), the teachers and students go through four main stages to complete the task.

Introducing the task and building knowledge of the field

In the first stage, the teacher guides students to understand what the task requires them to do. The teacher and students discuss the purpose, audience, genre, and content of the writing task. The students table this key information in a graphic organiser (see Fig. 9.2). This is posted to their digital portfolio.

Figure 9.1 Example Writing Task

Purpose	Audience	Genre	Content
Promotion – persuade people to visit Hong Kong	Tourists looking for somewhere to visit	Travel blog	Hong Kong attractions, transportation, activities

Figure 9.2 Example graphic organiser

Teachers and students then share what they know about the purpose, audience, genre, and content of the writing task. The teachers provide four guiding questions on Nearpod and provide a whiteboard slide for students to share their ideas collaboratively and simultaneously:

(1) What attractions and activities are there in Hong Kong?
(2) How can we persuade people to visit Hong Kong?
(3) Which countries might tourists come to Hong Kong from?
(4) What might we read or see in a travel blog?

The teachers predict that students will have the required content knowledge – information about Hong Kong attractions and activities – but there will be less genre knowledge – travel blogs. Therefore, for out-of-class learning, the teachers prepare a short video using Edpuzzle for students to learn about the key features, organisation, and style of travel blogs. A few questions are embedded in the video to keep the students engaged and assess their participation. The teachers provide links to some different travel blogs and encourage students to visit them, for example https://travelforkids.com and www.ytravelblog.com. Students are asked to post anything they learn about travel blogs to their portfolio on Canvas.

Modelling and deconstructing the genre

In the second stage, the teachers' aim is to build up students' understanding of the content, organisation, and language and style of travel blogs. They also inform students about the school-based writing criteria for different attainment milestones. They invite students to visit an authentic travel blog and look at the macro features, for example headings, photographs, videos, hyperlinks. They can take a screenshot and ask students to label it using Nearpod with the names of the macro features. Teachers and students then discuss the purpose of the different features. The teacher can ask questions like, "Why does a travel blog contain photographs?" or "Why are some words highlighted/coloured/bolded?" Next, the teachers focus on the micro features, specifically, a written part of the travel blog entry and analyse the language and style of the writing, for example the tenses used, if the writer writes in the first, second, or third person, or a mix, cohesive devices used, and salient features of travel blogs. Students are encouraged to make notes with examples from the model text for future reference. Students post the annotated text and notes to their portfolio.

Then, the teacher shows the school-based writing criteria for different attainment milestones. Students are encouraged to look back at their performance on their previous work in their portfolio and set individual goals for the current writing task using a template that they post in their portfolio. The teachers review their goals and provide feedback if necessary. After class, students are encouraged to visit the websites of the authentic travel blogs they have been provided (e.g. https://travelforkids.com and www.ytravelblog.com) and look at the macro and micro features again. A Padlet digital noticeboard is set up for students who have any questions to post them.

Joint construction

In the third stage, the teachers and students' attention turns to writing. However, it is the teacher who acts as the writer, with students contributing ideas, thoughts, and opinions to co-construct a text together. To select a topic to write about, the teachers and students do a quick poll to select one Hong Kong attraction. The teachers then show a graphic organiser on Nearpod with a few questions or prompts to stimulate discussion (see Figure 9.3). The teachers and students complete the graphic organiser together. If they do not know some necessary information, then they search for it on kiddle.com.

The teacher and students then use the information to co-construct the text. This is a dialogic process, with teachers eliciting ideas, students contributing, debating, and finally the teachers scribing them on a shared online document, such as Google Slides. Once the text is constructed, it can be uploaded to students' digital portfolios as a model for their independent writing (see Figure 9.4). They then use the school-based writing criteria to evaluate the text.

After the class, students are asked to select one attraction in Hong Kong to write about for the travel blog. They can do some research

What attraction?	What can people do there?	Why should people go there?	How can people get there?	How much does it cost?

Figure 9.3 Example graphic organiser for joint construction

> **Ocean Park**
>
> Ocean Park is one of the main attractions in Hong Kong. It has many things for people to do. You can ride on rollercoasters, a cable car, and a log flume. There are also pandas, sharks, and many other animals. You should definitely visit Ocean Park because there are things for everyone to do.
>
> You can get to Ocean Park by MTR. Get off at Ocean Park station. Park tickets start at HK$249 for children and HK$498 for adults. Visit www.oceanpark.com.hk/en for more information.

Figure 9.4 Example Co-Constructed Text

and complete a graphic organiser with the information they find on their attraction. They can post this in their digital portfolio.

Independent writing

In this stage, the students write their own travel blog entry. They can choose an attraction to write about and use the information in the graphic organiser as an aid to help them. Teachers remind students to spend time drafting, revising, and editing their work. Scaffolding such as peer feedback, conferencing, use of digital tools, such as Grammarly or WordHippo, and oral or written comments using Canvas are provided. Students are also reminded to look at the different resources they have compiled in their digital portfolio over the previous sessions.

The teachers compile the different travel blog entries and construct a class travel blog using Blogger. Students are asked to engage in self-reflection about their effort and satisfaction with their writing process and product. They should refer back to their task goals. Teachers then evaluate each entry and provide feedback based on the school-based writing criteria for different attainment milestones. The feedback is posted in students' digital portfolios to inform them of their attainment level.

The teachers engage in similar writing tasks throughout the six years of secondary education. The aim is to prepare students with knowledge of a variety of writing tasks of different genres. As the digital portfolio is used throughout the six years, the students can regularly look back at their previous work, use it as reference materials for current tasks or assessments, and evaluate their progress.

Strategies to blend assessment and learning of writing

The aforementioned example of the genre-based writing task shows how teachers in the school blend assessment and learning of writing using digital portfolios. The explicit nature of the genre-based approach means that teachers and learners can simultaneously consider the learning of writing and assessment of writing. For example while analysing an exemplar to build genre knowledge, teachers can also refer students to the assessment rubric. They can then notice both the genre features and the importance of these to their assessment grades. The following are some of the different ways the teachers in the school blend assessment and learning of writing.

Designing the writing task:

- Using public assessment tasks as catalysts for school-based writing tasks: To help students to connect the learning of writing with the public assessment, using public assessment tasks within the writing can help. Students can see the relationship between the assessment task and their in-class writing instruction and can gain a better understanding of the assessment expectations. An archive of public assessment writing tasks can be created on the LMS for student reference and self-directed learning.

Continuously contributing to the digital portfolio:

- Storing and organising jointly completed activities and co-constructed texts: During the writing process, the teachers and learners jointly complete activities and co-construct texts together. These become important reference materials for students as they engage in their independent writing. Storing them in their digital portfolios recognises the shared ownership of the texts and provides them with exemplars for their own writing. These texts can be compared to the assessment criteria – helping learners notice the relationship between the text and criteria.
- Storing and organising student independent writing: As students construct their own texts, these can also be stored in their digital portfolio.

Developing self-access resources:

- Providing teacher-made videos with activities and tasks: As class time can be limited, and students have multiple language

proficiencies, providing short videos about a writing skill, content or genre can help learners develop important knowledge they need to complete the writing task. Using a video-hosting site like Edpuzzle can be useful to monitor students' participation and performance.
- Uploading exemplar texts with assessment feedback: Teachers can create an archive of previous written texts composed by students or teachers, with associated assessment feedback. Students can get a better understanding of the quality of work in relation to the assessment criteria of the task.

Linking school-based writing criteria with public assessment criteria:

- Developing a school-based writing criteria for different attainment milestones: As writing takes a long time to master, it is good to provide a framework to help inform students of their attainment. This allows them to set goals and evaluate their own performance. The criteria can be used throughout the writing tasks to strengthen the relationship between learning and assessment.

Engaging in continuous formative assessment and feedback:

- Identifying knowledge gaps: Teachers do not have time to prepare students with all the knowledge they need for every writing task. Teachers can help students identify gaps in the knowledge they need to complete a task successfully and be given suggestions on how to fill them.
- Self-, peer, and teacher feedback: Throughout the writing process, and across different writing tasks, students should be given opportunities to assess their own and their peers' writing. Ways to assess and give feedback can be demonstrated on co-constructed texts or exemplars. The feedback can be included in the digital portfolio to help students reflect and feed the feedback forward.

Importantly, teachers need to remember the goal when blending assessment and learning is that they complement each other. This requires teachers to continuously refer to the assessment task and criteria but also make sure students are making progress in the knowledge and skills they need for writing.

Principles of using digital portfolios with secondary school language learners

The vignette demonstrates how one secondary school has used a digital portfolio programme to blend the learning and assessment of writing. Throughout a writing task, teachers and students are continuously engaging in learning and assessment. This ensures students are informed of the task expectations and can develop their own learning goals, they have the knowledge and resources to complete the task effectively and can see the connection between the school-based writing task and the external public assessments. The following are some principles that might guide you to develop your own digital portfolio programme in a secondary school language classroom:

> **Principle 1: Align school-based writing tasks, digital portfolio, and public assessment tasks:** It is likely that public assessments will require students to demonstrate specific writing skills and be able to construct a variety of genres for different audiences. Teachers can review the public assessment aims and materials and take reference to them when designing writing tasks. They can even upload the aims and assessment rubrics of the public exam writing tasks to the students' digital portfolios for their reference.
>
> **Principle 2: Integrate different digital tools with the digital portfolio:** Some learning management platforms, such as Canvas, allow the integration of other digital tools. This can mean there is one central place where students can access the materials and resources they need to complete their writing tasks.
>
> **Principle 3: Utilise in- and out-of-class time effectively and appropriately:** Some tasks are best completed at school while others can be completed at home. Teachers can create short videos for students to access at home, and this can release class time for joint text construction or independent writing.
>
> **Principle 4: Make attainment milestones transparent:** For students to stay motivated and see progress in their abilities, it is important that they are made aware of their abilities and have clear attainment milestones. Teachers can refer to government and assessment documents, such as the Hong Kong LPF, when formulating attainment milestones.

Conclusion

This chapter has presented important considerations and challenges of preparing secondary school learners for high-stakes public writing assessments. It has suggested how technology, and specifically the use of a digital portfolio, can be integrated into a writing task to help connect school-based tasks with public assessments.

While ensuring amble preparation for public assessments is likely be a major concern for secondary school students and their teachers, we need to remember that writing in the real world and writing for a test are very different and require different skills. Tests require students to write within a time limit without much opportunity to prepare and no opportunity to engage in research. The writing purpose and audience are contrived. Real-life writing, on the other hand, is purposeful. We know why we are writing and to whom, and this will guide the genre we choose, our style, tone, and even effort. It is a much more considered and carefully thought-out process. As teachers, we need to make this distinction clear to learners and help them develop the knowledge and skills needed for test writing and real-world writing.

Discussion questions

After reading the chapter, discuss and consider the following questions to help consolidate your understanding and connect what you are learning to your own classroom or future classroom.

1 What are the challenges of teaching secondary school language learners?
2 How might we blend the evaluation and learning of writing via digital portfolios?
3 Why might public writing assessments be a good catalyst for school-based writing task?
4 Why is it important to prepare students for both writing assessment tasks and real-world writing tasks?
5 Can you think of any other principles that could help you when developing a school-based digital portfolio programme?

Resources

The following is a list of digital tools and platforms mentioned in this chapter:

Edpuzzle

Edpuzzle is a video hosting site that allows teachers to embed questions and prompts into a video. Teachers can monitor students' participation, engagement, and performance. Visit: edpuzzle.com

Nearpod

Nearpod is an interactive presentation software. Teachers can create a presentation that students can follow and interact with on their own devices. Visit: nearpod.com

Canvas

Canvas is an LMS with integrated tools to help teachers and students manage, monitor, and interact around learning activities and tasks. Digital portfolios are linked to a student's account and not the teacher, so it can move with them as they progress through secondary school and graduate. Visit: www.instructure.com

natgeokids.com

natgeokids.com is a website owned by National Geographic. It provides articles, videos, and other resources and activities aimed at children. Visit: natgeokids.com

Google Translate

Google Translate is a web-based translation tool. Visit: https://translate.google.com

Quizizz

Quizizz is an interactive quiz platform that teachers can use to make classes quizzes. It provides analytics on student performance which can help teachers provide formative feedback instantly. Visit: https://quizizz.com

Padlet

Padlet is an interactive noticeboard where teachers and students can post, collaborate, and interact in real time. Visit: https://padlet.com

Kiddle

Kiddle is a child-friendly search engine designed by Google for children. It is a safe environment for student research. Visit: kiddle.com

Blogger

Blogger is a web-based blog platform developed by Google. Teachers can create a class blog where students' work can be uploaded and commented on. The blog can be closed or open depending on the audience of the blog. Visit: blogger.com

References

Becker, C. (2015). Assessment and portfolios. In J. Bland (Ed.), *Teaching English to young learners: Critical issues in language teaching with 3–12 year olds*. Bloomsbury.

Costley, T. (2018). Learning as adolescents. In A. Burns & J. C. Richards (Eds.), *The Cambridge guide to learning English as a second language*. Cambridge University Press.

Curriculum Development Council. (2017). *English language education: Key learning area curriculum guide (primary 1 – secondary 6)*. Curriculum Development Council.

Hawe, E., & Dixon, H. (2017). Assessment for learning: A catalyst for student self-regulation. *Assessment & Evaluation in Higher Education*, *42*(8), 1181–1192.

Hess, N. (2001). *Teaching large multilevel classes*. Cambridge University Press.

Hong Kong Examinations and Assessment Authority (2022). *Hong Kong Diploma of Secondary Education Examination: Assessment framework*. https://www.hkeaa.edu.hk/en/hkdse/assessment/assessment_framework/

Ryan, A. M., & Patrick, H. (2001). The classroom social environment and changes in adolescents' motivation and engagement during middle school. *American Educational Research Journal*, *38*(2), 437–460.

Stickler, U. (2022). *Technology and language teaching*. Cambridge University Press.

Tragant, E., & Victori, M. (2006). Reported strategy use and age. In C. Muñoz (Ed.), *Age and the rate of foreign language learning* (pp. 208–236). Multilingual Matters.

10 Future Directions

Book summary

The book starts with a concise introduction, which outlines the purpose, audience, and usage of the book. This is followed by ten chapters. Chapter 1 provides basic definitions and examples of both paper-based and digital portfolios and discusses an evolution of digital portfolios in education over the past two decades. Chapter 2 describes the theory of socio-constructivism, which unpacks the rationale for digital portfolios. The theory refers to how students engage in an iterative meaning-making process through portfolio compilation reflectively and collaboratively. It discusses the nitty-gritty of digital portfolios, such as features, types, and medium. Chapter 2 further reviews state-of-the-art literature on the pros and cons of adopting digital portfolios for writing instruction and their effectiveness in terms of motivation enhancement, acquisition of metacognitive composing skills, and gains in academic outcomes.

Chapter 3 focuses on the ways digital portfolios can be seamlessly integrated into three writing instructional approaches. It introduces three curriculum integration methods, which facilitate the application of digital portfolios in diverse writing classroom contexts. The chapter continues to illustrate a tried-and-tested curriculum design framework proposed by the first author. The practicality of incorporating the portfolio approach in writing classrooms is critically evaluated. Chapter 4 discusses four purposes of writing assessment and distinguishes between classroom-based versus large-scale digital portfolio assessment. It illustrates how teachers can utilise digital portfolios to carry out assessment of/for/as learning in the writing classrooms. The chapter also describes the procedures of rubric construction for digital portfolio assessment.

Chapter 5 is about the role of feedback in portfolio assessment and digital portfolios. It first unpacks the conceptualisation of e-feedback from three perspectives. Chapter 5 then instructs how teachers can integrate e-feedback into portfolios via various sources, modes, and technology types. It further introduces a four-step model concerning how teachers can guide students to develop self-regulated learning through engaging in e-feedback dialogically and metacognitively. Chapter 6 is about digital portfolio application tools. It first talks about the rise of digital tools. Then, the chapter describes the five principles to help teachers select the right tool for their portfolio programmes. After that, it discusses three common digital portfolio platforms. Lastly, Chapter 6 reviews three popular digital portfolio applications by looking into their strengths and limitations.

Chapters 7, 8, and 9 are practical-oriented sections, which describe three contextualised vignettes emphasising various stages of schooling and different aspects of language development. Chapter 7, aka Vignette 1, is about how digital portfolios foster young learners' literacy development in pre-school settings. Chapter 8, aka Vignette 2, is about how the implementation of digital portfolios promotes self-regulated learning in writing in primary school contexts. Chapter 9, aka Vignette 3, is about the productive synergy between assessment and learning of writing in secondary school environments. Each scenario-based chapter presents in the following sequence: an introduction, the school, the digital portfolio programme, principles of using digital portfolios with pre-school/primary/secondary learners, discussion questions, and resources. These three chapters provide readers with an up-to-date, authentic, and pragmatic stance when they attempt digital portfolios. Chapter 10 is about future directions of digital portfolios when used as an instructional approach. The next part discusses how to advance writing instruction with digital portfolios.

Use of digital portfolios to advance writing instruction

Since digital portfolios are a medium, a technology, a pedagogy, an assessment, and a catalyst for effective language instruction, they play multiple roles in promoting a community of practice wherein students' writing development can be made visible, transferable, and sustainable (Eynon & Gambino, 2017). As discussed in the previous chapters, digital portfolios have great potential to advance writing instruction by shifting the emphasis from teachers to learners, outcomes to experience, products to processes, and standard compliance to knowledge creation (Segaran & Hasim, 2021). In writing classrooms, digital portfolios can help students develop: (1) a unique student writer identity; (2) learner autonomy; (3) personalised learning experience; (4) an authorial voice; and (5) a positive self-efficacy belief (Navarre, 2019). Putting students at the centre of learning writing appears to be the first priority in digital portfolios. The following space provides suggestions on how to advance writing pedagogy from teachers' and students' perspectives.

Teachers

Teachers can adopt digital portfolios as a curricular component (cf. Chapter 3), an assessment method (cf. Chapter 4), and a technological medium (cf. Chapter 6) to advance writing instruction. To merge with the existing curriculum, teachers can utilise digital portfolios to carry out either process-oriented or genre-based writing approaches by encouraging students to compose their drafts in stages. Since digital portfolios enable learners to perform self- and peer assessment regularly, these learning-oriented activities create ample opportunities for students to improve their writing over time and in a low-stakes online environment (Pourdana & Tavassoli, 2022). Launching digital portfolios alongside the pre-existing curriculum is likely to reduce teachers' workload and anxiety. After all, the classroom application of digital portfolios has been part of online instruction.

If teachers make use of digital portfolios as authentic assessment, they can diagnose students' strengths and weaknesses in writing more accurately and constantly through observations, dialogues, and timely feedback (cf. Chapter 5). On most digital portfolio software, teachers can check on students' academic achievements and use those assessment data to fine-tune their writing instruction accordingly. While summative portfolio scoring is complicated to perform, using digital portfolios to assess student writing formatively (e.g. provision of audio/video-based teacher feedback to facilitate text revision) would be a step forward (Lam, 2021).

Employing digital portfolios as a powerful medium for remote instruction or flipped teaching is high on the agenda. The functions of homework submission, collection, reflection, and management in digital portfolio tools transform students into autonomous learners during class suspension owing to natural disasters, warfare, or public health crises like the COVID-19 pandemic (Daniel, 2020). With much unpredictability in the near future, teachers can use digital portfolios as a dynamic platform to complement in-person teaching for saving precious instructional hours as well as promoting learner independence outside brick-and-mortar school campuses (Sasai, 2017).

Students

Regarding student learning, digital portfolios support collaboration, reflection, and motivation in writing. As said previously (Chapter 6), digital portfolios, particularly via online word processors or web-based editing systems, promote collaborative writing tasks, project-based assignments, and peer editing/assessment activities which allow students to work in teams and enhance their communicative competence to be future-ready (Rabbani Yekta & Kana'ni, 2020). This collaborative culture dovetails with the idea of socio-constructivism, which highlights co-construction of knowledge and interdependence of portfolio-based learning, especially within web-based digital portfolio contexts (Sun & Yang, 2015). The social connection among peers in digital portfolios increases student confidence in writing and digital presence in their online learning.

Undoubtedly, reflection is the key to portfolio-based learning. By compiling and constructing their digital portfolios, students have sufficient opportunities to review their artefacts, achievements, and learning trajectories metacognitively. The acts of reflection in digital portfolios align well with portfolio-thinking, where interactive and inquisitive evaluation of one's own portfolio works is deemed indispensable (Bowman et al., 2016). Anyhow, helping students to engage in reflective practices via digital portfolio compilation is likely to equip them with one of the most significant twenty-first-century study skills – learning-how-to-learn for their study or professional careers (Wang & Lee, 2021).

More importantly, digital portfolios are likely to enhance student writing motivation. It is because besides texts, students can freely express their views and voices through other multimodal artefacts with which they feel familiar, namely video, audio, and graphics (Aygün & Aydin, 2016). Students can complete their digital compositions in their portfolios with a broad range of learning evidence by inserting an audio reflective file, a hyperlink to scientific facts, or PowerPoint slides showcasing best results. If school-based portfolio platforms include games-based learning elements, students are even more motivated to participate in portfolio works (Cho, 2018). The subsequent part delineates possible caveats about digital portfolio implementation.

Caveats about digital portfolio implementation

Although digital portfolios bring hope to educationalists and learners, they are not a panacea for all language teaching problems. In fact, scholars have identified that when teachers introduce digital portfolios in their workplaces, certain challenges remain unresolved and perhaps perpetual, such as (a) the digital divide, (b) digital literacy, (c) privacy issues, (d) tensions with an audit culture, and (e) student engagement.

The digital divide

While students were born and live in the digital age, it does not necessarily mean that all students have equal access to computer gadgets and

Internet-related infrastructure to facilitate e-learning. Oftentimes, teachers may take for granted that when they carry out digital portfolios or other e-pedagogy initiatives, students could benefit from this education technology. In reality, certain socioeconomically disadvantaged students cannot afford those basic digital tools, such as tablets, laptops, mobiles, not to mention those pricey data subscription plans for stable Wi-Fi connection when using web-based application tools at home. Although most schools provide students with tablets and free campus Wi-Fi, less-privileged students cannot continue to complete and compile their digital tasks at home. The digital divide in language education has long been documented (Hockly & Dudeney, 2018). Scholars have warned that digital portfolios and similar e-learning approaches may create inequality in education, especially for those who have limited access to technology in either rural areas or underdeveloped countries (Rafalow & Puckett, 2022).

Digital literacy

To warrant effective digital portfolio implementation, teachers and students are expected to reach a certain level of digital literacy (Cummins & Davesne, 2009). Students need to know how to upload and download their digital artefacts and give and receive peer e-feedback on a learning management system proficiently. Although most students are tech-savvy, one study shows that some of these students only know how to email to friends, use word processors, and surf the Internet for entertainment (Derounian, 2020). More advanced functions of digital portfolios remain challenging to them. Likewise, some teachers may need specific computer training before they are ready to try out digital portfolios. Research shows that teacher reluctance to adopt this instructional approach is due to their lack of confidence, readiness, and capability in computer literacy (Wuetherick & Dickinson, 2015). Without sufficient knowledge and skills, teachers may find it exacting to launch, develop, and even sustain their digital portfolio programmes for more than one academic year and across various subject disciplines (Bryant & Chittum, 2013).

Privacy issues

Digital portfolios are stored in a shared domain, especially of weblog-based and website-supported digital portfolios. It is possible that students' artefacts and digital reflective pieces are discernible in the public eye. Simply put, students' privacy has no guarantee. Students may become vulnerable to doxxing and cyberbullying (Wilson et al., 2018). Because of this, students' mental well-being and psychological state may suffer if they are subjected to negative experiences online. For young pupils aged below nine, their privacy is somewhat easily infringed as they are not mature enough to have awareness unless informed by their parents and teachers. However, for senior grade students, they could be explicitly taught what or what not to be uploaded and published on the digital portfolio platform to protect their confidentiality and student identity, such as certain sensitive data relating to family, health, gender, and aptitude. Personal particulars are not appropriate to be shown in students' digital dossiers either, like email address, mobile number, and social media accounts to avoid unnecessary cyberstalking or scams.

Tensions with an audit culture

Because of the rise of an audit culture in education, student learning has to be made accountable to key stakeholders. Principals and teachers are under pressure to train students to obtain outstanding results in the public exams, so that schools can avoid sanction or closure. Against this backdrop, digital portfolios are deemed a promising tool to raise students' academic standards, given that this instructional approach promotes knowledge transfer, metacognition, and collaborative learning. These formative assessment practices are primarily measured by narratives, observations, or dialogues (via conferences) in a learning-oriented culture. Situated in an exam-oriented culture, scoring digital portfolios with standardised content, layout, type, and quantity of artefacts appears to be inevitable although such *top-down* portfolios are likely to weaken their formative functions (Barrett, 2007). In reality, digital portfolios featuring process writing, originality, and experiential learning run counter to the audit culture, which requires students and teachers to comply with a set of externally imposed assessment criteria strictly. In that sense, *bottom-up* portfolios possibly have tensions with an accountability system.

Student engagement

Digital portfolios can help students improve writing ability, learning motivation, and self-efficacy (Yancey, 2019). That said, without student active participation, it is taxing to materialise these educational benefits even though teachers launch a comprehensive digital portfolio programme. Researchers have long found that students were snowed under with portfolio tasks, experienced boredom with portfolio compilation, and felt unmotivated to engage in revising digital texts (Aydin, 2014). In certain contexts, digital portfolios are perceived as an assignment collection system, in which the role of students is reduced to content suppliers. If teachers do not engage students in a digital portfolio programme pedagogically, students cannot develop a full sense of agency, belonging, and achievements they take pride in. The use of selected-response items, box-ticking exercises, and solo writing tasks will definitely restrict students from exploiting the multimodal attribute of digital portfolios, such as having students to peer edit a piece of work on Google Docs or to draft a wiki page by researching a celebrity on Instagram and YouTube in groups. The following part presents future trends of digital portfolios and their educational potential.

Future trends of digital portfolios and their educational values

To date, digital portfolio scholarship has largely focused on the effectiveness of implementation and students' academic outcomes after their exposure to a portfolio programme for a short period, for example one school semester. This research evidence is robust and trustworthy, but it does not develop a forward-looking and localised understanding of how frontline teachers attempt the digital portfolio approach from their perspectives. Because of this, the ensuing paragraphs provide readers with pointers to consider when they initiate their digital portfolio programmes, conduct school-based action research projects, and collaborate with university teachers on funded digital portfolio-based projects.

Affective aspects: management, emotion, and motivation

Teachers can study how students manage their e-portfolios over time because they usually assess students' digital portfolios as a product not as a process. By exploring learner portfolio management experience, teachers can resolve possible impeding factors that stand in the way of digital portfolio implementation. Understanding student emotional state is another future direction, given that not much attention is paid to how students respond to digital portfolio-based learning affectively (Lam, 2022). Although most portfolio studies report positive findings like improved accuracy of writing, it does not mean that students show preference over or enjoy the digital portfolio process, especially when they have little or no say in those studies. Getting to know how student emotional state may influence the success or failure of digital portfolio construction would be an up-and-coming trend. It is evident that students with higher motivation tend to compile their digital portfolios more effectively and vice versa (Baas et al., 2020). Nevertheless, teachers probably have no idea of what triggers student motivation to create their digital portfolios. Teachers are perhaps interested to know why some students are more motivated than others regarding portfolio content compilation in terms of grade level (particularly in junior grades), gender, ethnicity, self-efficacy, family background, and medium of instruction.

Technical aspects: types, platforms, and transition

Research has introduced numerous digital portfolio tools, including blogs, customised portfolio application software, and websites (cf. Chapter 6). Yet, these practically oriented reports simply provide basic descriptions of how these tools are applied in the classroom contexts. To help teachers make informed decisions, researchers may consider administering a large-scale survey that investigate transnational students' perceptions and experiences of using designated digital portfolio tools at various grade levels. Such questionnaire findings are likely to advance digital portfolio scholarship. More recently, there are studies exploring the effectiveness of adopting social media as digital portfolio platforms to enhance student writing (i.e. Facebook; Aydin, 2014; Barrot, 2021). Nonetheless, teachers may not possess sufficient understanding of whether other social media platforms and instant messaging apps would have comparable benefits, namely Instagram, TikTok, Twitter, WhatsApp, or Telegram if they employ those tools in their workplaces. Another future trend of digital portfolios is the transition from paper-based to digital portfolio programmes. Scholars may look into how teachers manipulate such a significant transformation, particularly in a localised context where support and infrastructure remain scarce. These classroom data are essential to provide teachers with updated input if they aspire to overhaul their portfolio programmes electronically.

Professional aspects: assessment literacy, training, and identity

One up-and-coming trend of digital portfolios is to develop stakeholders' digital portfolio assessment literacy. Teachers and students need essential knowledge and skills to operate digital portfolios. For teachers, they need a thorough conceptualisation of what digital portfolios entail and technical know-how to fulfil formative and summative assessment purposes. For students, they need to attain a certain level of computer literacy (manipulation of portfolio interfaces and keyboarding skills) and understand how digital portfolios can help improve writing, such as accuracy (mobilising online resources like grammar-checkers; Yancey, 2019). The successful uptake of digital portfolio assessment literacy requires training. During the pandemic, there has been no shortage of professional workshops, including webinars, virtual lecture series, and free international conferences involving digital portfolio applications. Because of this, another future trend of digital portfolios is to provide teachers with assessment training through online courses, publications (textbooks and journal articles), and podcasts with a theme on digital portfolios. Lastly, scholars may investigate the role of teachers-as-assessors within digital portfolio programmes. It is because teachers usually do not feel comfortable with their identity as an evaluator as compared to their identity as a language coach when performing alternative assessments (Looney et al., 2017). Examining the new role of teachers-as-assessors in the digital portfolio process could be another forthcoming trend. The penultimate part presents a self-evaluation task, which gives readers a quick recap on the book.

Self-evaluation task

Please answer the following questions by referring to the previous chapters if necessary.

1 Which chapter do I find most practical and insightful? Why?
2 What instructional benefits of digital portfolios can I apply in my prospective or current classroom context? In what ways can these benefits advance writing instruction in various educational settings?
3 Based upon a pre-service teacher's perspective, what preparation do I need if I plan to introduce digital portfolios in my teaching practicum?
4 How do I persuade the principal if I want to initiate a digital writing portfolio programme as an instructional approach in one Grade 10 class? (Hint: *making a three-minute mini speech when I talk to the principal*.)
5 In Chapters 7–9, which vignette is most relevant to my teacher training background and educational context? What lessons can I learn from this vignette and how do I overcome some of the challenges experienced by those teachers?
6 Concerning the future trends of digital portfolios, which one is worth investigation? Why?

Conclusion

Chapter 10 has summarised the whole monograph chapter by chapter. It then suggests how to use digital portfolios to advance writing instruction from teachers' and students' perspectives. After that, it discussed five caveats about digital portfolio implementation, including the digital divide, digital literacy, privacy issues, tensions with an audit culture, and student engagement. Next, the chapter presented three major future trends of digital portfolios, such as affective aspects (portfolio management, student emotion, and learning motivation), technical aspects (preferred portfolio types, digital portfolio platforms, and transition from paper-based to digital portfolio programmes), and professional aspects (assessment literacy development, assessment training, and teachers-as-assessors identities). Lastly, the chapter ended with a self-evaluation task.

References

Aydin, S. (2014). EFL writers' attitudes and perceptions towards F-portfolio use. *TechTrends*, *58*(2), 59–77.

Aygün, S., & Aydin, S. (2016). The use of e-portfolio in EFL writing: A review of literature. *ELT Research Journal*, *5*(3), 205–217.

Baas, D., Vermeulen, M., Castelijns, J., Martens, R., & Segers, M. (2020). Portfolios as a tool for AfL and student motivation: Are they related? *Assessment in Education: Principles, Policy & Practice*, *27*(4), 444–462.

Barrett, H. C. (2007). Researching electronic portfolios and learner engagement: The REFLECT initiative. *Journal of Adolescent & Adult Literacy*, *50*(6), 436–449.

Barrot, J. S. (2021). Effects of Facebook-based e-Portfolio on ESL learners' writing performance. *Language, Culture and Curriculum*, *34*(1), 95–111.

Bowman, J., Lowe, B., Sabourin, K., & Sweet, C. (2016). The use of ePortfolios to support metacognitive practice in a first-year writing program. *International Journal of ePortfolio*, *6*(1), 1–22.

Bryant, L. H., & Chittum, J. R. (2013). ePortfolio effectiveness: A(n ill-fated) search for empirical support. *International Journal of ePortfolio*, *3*(2), 189–198.

Cho, H. (2018). The pitfalls and promises of electronic portfolio assessment with secondary English language learners. In J. Perren, K. B. Kelch, J. Byun, S. Cervantes, & S. Safari (Eds.), *Applications of CALL theory in ESL and EFL environments* (pp. 111–129). IGI Global.

Cummins, P. W., & Davesne, C. (2009). Using electronic portfolios for second language assessment. *The Modern Language Journal*, *93*, 848–867.

Daniel, S. J. (2020). Education and the COVID-19 pandemic. *Prospects*, 1–6.

Derounian, J. G. (2020). Mobiles in class? *Active Learning in Higher Education*, *21*(2), 142–153.

Eynon, B., & Gambino, L. M. (2017). *High-impact ePortfolio practice: A catalyst for student, faculty, and institutional learning*. Stylus Publishing.

Hockly, N., & Dudeney, G. (2018). Current and future digital trends in ELT. *RELC Journal*, *49*(2), 164–178.

Lam, R. (2021). Using ePortfolios to promote assessment of, for, as learning in EFL writing. *The European Journal of Applied Linguistics and TEFL*, *10*(1), 101–120.

Lam, R. (2022). E-portfolios: What we know, what we don't, and what we need to know. *RELC Journal*. https://doi.org/10.1177/0033688220974102

Looney, A., Cumming, J., van Der Kleij, F., & Harris, K. (2017). Reconceptualising the role of teachers as assessors: Teacher assessment identity. *Assessment in Education: Principles, Policy & Practice*, *25*(5), 442–467.

Navarre, A. (2019). *Technology-enhanced teaching and learning of Chinese as a foreign language* (1st ed., Vol. 1). Routledge.

Pourdana, N., & Tavassoli, K. (2022). Differential impacts of e-portfolio assessment on language learners' engagement modes and genre-based writing improvement. *Language Testing in Asia, 12*(7). https://doi.org/10.1186/s40468-022-00156-7

Rabbani Yekta, R., & Kana'ni, M. A. (2020). Using Google Drive as the e-Portfolio for the self-assessment of speaking fluency. *International Journal of Research in English Education, 5*(2), 49–60.

Rafalow, M. H., & Puckett, C. (2022). Sorting machines: Digital technology and categorical inequality in education. *Educational Researcher, 51*(4), 274–278.

Sasai, L. (2017). Self-regulated learning and the use of online portfolios: A social cognitive perspective. *Journal of Educational and Social Research, 7*(2), 55–65.

Segaran, M. K., & Hasim, Z. (2021). Self-regulated learning through ePortfolio: A meta-analysis. *Malaysian Journal of Learning and Instruction, 18*(1), 131–156.

Sun, Y. C., & Yang, F. Y. (2015). I help, therefore, I learn: Service learning on web 2.0 in an EFL speaking class. *Computer Assisted Language Learning, 28*(3), 202–219.

Wang, L., & Lee, I. (2021). L2 learners' agentic engagement in an assessment as learning-focused writing classroom. *Assessing Writing, 50*, 100571.

Wilson, C., Slade, C., Kirby, M., Downer, T., Fisher, M., & Nuessler, S. (2018). Digital ethics and the use of ePortfolio: A scoping review of the literature. *International Journal of ePortfolio, 8*(2), 115–125.

Wuetherick, B., & Dickinson, J. (2015). Why ePortfolios? Student perceptions of ePortfolio use in continuing education learning environments. *International Journal of ePortfolio, 5*(1), 39–53.

Yancey, K. B. (Ed.). (2019). *ePortfolio as curriculum: Models and practices for developing students' ePortfolio literacy*. Stylus Publishing.

Useful Platforms, Apps, and Digital Tools

The following is a list of platforms, apps, and digital tools introduced in the book. They are organised by the chapter they are first mentioned.

Chapter 1*

    Edmodo   https://new.edmodo.com/
    Google Sites   https://sites.google.com/
    REFLECT Initiatives http://electronicportfolios.org/reflect/
    Wiki   https://en.wikipedia.org/wiki/Wikipedia:How_to_create_a_page

Some common digital tools, briefly introduced in Chapter 1 will appear in later chapters.

Chapter 2

    Audacity   www.audacityteam.org/
    e-Rater   www.ets.org/erater
    ePEARL   www.epearl.co.uk
    Facebook   https://facebook.com
    Instagram   www.instagram.com
    Jing aka Snagit www.techsmith.com/screen-capture.html
    Microsoft Office 365 (PowerPoint, One note, Teams) www.microsoft.com
    Wix   www.wix.com
    WordPress   https://wordpress.com

Chapter 3

e-Class www.eclass.com.hk
G Suite (Google classroom, Jamboard, G-mail) https://workspace.google.com
Grammarly www.grammarly.com
Moodle https://moodle.com
Padlet https://padlet.com
Wordtune www.wordtune.com
Zoom https://zoom.us

Chapter 4

Schoology www.powerschool.com/solutions/unified-classroom/schoology-learning/

Chapter 5

My Story Book Maker www.mystorybook.com
Pictello www.assistiveware.com/products/pictello
Pigai http://en.pigai.org
WeChat www.wechat.com
WhatsApp www.whatsapp.com
YouTube www.youtube.com

Chapter 6

Blackboard www.blackboard.com
Blogger www.blogger.com/
Canvas www.instructure.com/canvas
ClassDojo www.classdojo.com
Edublogs https://edublogs.org
FreshGrade https://freshgrade.com
Mahara https://mahara.org
Quizlet https://quizlet.com/en-gb
Seesaw https://web.seesaw.me/lessons

Chapter 7

Wordwall https://wordwall.net

Chapter 8

WordHippo   www.wordhippo.com

Chapter 9

Edpuzzle   https://edpuzzle.com
Google Translate   https://translate.google.com
Kiddle   www.kiddle.co
natgeokids.com   https://kids.nationalgeographic.com
Nearpod   https://nearpod.com
Quizizz   https://quizizz.com/?fromBrowserLoad=true

Chapter 10

TikTok   www.tiktok.com
Twitter   https://twitter.com/?lang=en
Telegram   https://telegram.org/

Index

Note: Page numbers in *italics* indicate a figure and page numbers in **bold** indicate a table on the corresponding page.

accessibility and digital portfolios 16
affective aspects of digital portfolios 138–139
Al-Mutairi, A. S. R. 17
Al-Qallaf, C. L. 17
Alves, R. A. 43
analytic scoring 45–46, **49**
applications *see* tools, digital portfolio
artefacts 13, 40
assessment *as* learning (AAL) 41–45, *45*
assessment *for* learning (AFL) 41–45, *45*
assessment *of* learning (AOL) 41–45, *45*
assessment portfolios 14, **15**;
  assessment of/for/as learning using 41–45, *45*; feedback in 54–55;
  mini-research task on 50–51;
  portfolio pedagogy and 37–38;
  rubric construction for 45–50, **47–49**; for writing evaluation 38–41, **40**
audience 13–14
audio feedback 57–58
audit culture 137
authentic learning 11
Aydin, S. 17–18
Aygün, S. 17

Baas, D. 17
Blackboard 67

blending assessment and learning of writing in secondary school language classrooms: aligning school-based English-language writing assessments and public assessments and 119–120; digital portfolio programme for 120–121; example writing tasks for 121–125; introduction to 116–127; principles of using digital portfolios for 128; resources on 130–131; school setting for 118–119; strategies for 126–127
Blogger 67–68, 71–72, 114, 131
blogging tools 6
blogs 58, 67–68, 71–72
bottom-up processing skills development 87, 89–92, *91–92*
British Council 98

Canvas 67, 120–121, 130
Chau, J. 17–18
Cheng, G. 17–18
Chong, I. 59
ClassDojo 74, 76–77
classroom-based digital portfolio assessment (CBPA) 39, **40**
collaborative learning 68–69
collection 3
Connect to Learning Network 31
COVID-19 pandemic 30, 74, 78, 134, 139–140
curation 13

curriculum, digital portfolio-based: case study on 34–35; content and delivery in 29–30; context of writing instruction in 24–25; criteria in 30; design framework for 27–31, *28*; evaluation in 31; integration into traditional curriculum 25–27; monitoring in 30–31; practicality of 31–33; purpose in 29 customised portfolio applications 71–73

Dann, R. 44
Daskalogiannaki, E. 17
De Bruin, H. L. 17
Delett, J. S. 29
design framework for digital portfolio-based curriculum 27–31, *28*
digital divide 135–136
digital identity 14
digital literacy 16, 69, 136
digital natives 69
digital portfolios: advancing writing instruction using 24–25, 133–135; affective aspects of 138–139; applications of 5; for assessment (*see* assessment portfolios); audit culture and 137; for blending assessment and learning of writing in secondary school language classrooms 116–131; book summary of 132–133; caveats about implementation of 135–138; curriculum based on (*see* curriculum, digital portfolio-based); digital divide and 135–136; digital literacy and 16, 69, 136; effectiveness of 17–19; evidence-based 13; evolution of 5–8, *6*; facilitating pre-school learners' literacy development 86–99; feedback in (*See* e-feedback); in feedback-rich environments 13; future trends of 138–140; as learner-centred 13; literature review on 16–19; as multimodal 13; origin, features, types, and medium of 12–15, *13*, **15**; *versus* print portfolios 3–4, *4*; privacy issues with 136–137;

professional aspects of 139–140; pros and cons of 16–17; for self-regulated learning in writing of primary school learners 100–114; student engagement and 137–138; technical aspects of 58, 139; theoretical rationale for 10–11, *12*; three types of 14, **15**, 71–74; tools for (*See* tools, digital portfolio)

e-feedback 54–55; as-a-dialogue 55–56; audio 57–58; conceptualisation of 55–56; digital storytelling and 60–62; integrated into portfolios 56–58; as internal driver 56; as message or gift 55; modes of 57–58; in portfolio assessment 54–55; sharing of 60–61; taxonomy of technologies in 58; techniques to promote self-regulated learning with 58–62
Edpuzzle 130
Edublogs 72
effectiveness of digital portfolios 17–19
English across the curriculum (EAC) approach 32
English language curriculum, traditional 25–27
enquiry-based learning 31–32
ePEARL 18
European Language Portfolio (ELP) 113
evidence-based digital portfolios 13
Eynon, B. 31

Facebook 58, 139
feedback *See* e-feedback
feedback-rich environments, digital portfolios in 13
FreshGrade 67, 71–74, 77–78

Gambino, L. M. 31
General Certificate of Secondary Education (GCSE), U.K. 41
genre-based writing classrooms 32–33
Golonka, E. W. 58
Google Classroom 26, 60, 74–75, 89, 105, 114

Google Docs 44, 57–60, 68, 70, 75, 138
Google Drive 14, 60
Google Forms 44, 75
Google Jamboard 75, 105, 113–114
Google Keep 75
Google Meet 75
Google Sheets 75
Google Sites 73
Google Slides 75, 105
Google Translate 130
Google Workspace for Education 74–76
Graham, S. 43
Grammarly 58

Hand, R. 67
Händel, M. 19
holistic scoring 45–47, **47–48**
Hong Kong Diploma of Secondary Education (HKDSE) Examinations for English Language and Literature in English 119
hypertexts 5, 60

identity, digital 14
Instagram 138–139
instant messaging 58, 60
interactive whiteboards 58
iPads 14

James, M. 11

Kahoot 66
Kiddle 131

Lam, R. 27, 35, 41, 44
learner-centred digital portfolios 13
learning management systems 58, 60, 66–67, 88–89, 105, 110–111, 120–121
learning progression framework (LPF) 120
Lee, I. 41
literacy development in pre-schoolers: bottom-up processing skills in 87, 89–92, *91–92*; digital portfolio programme for 88–89; introduction to 86–92; parental involvement on Seesaw and 95–96; preparing students for use of Seesaw for 95; principles of using digital portfolios for 96–97; resources on 98–99; school setting for 88; top-down processing skills in 87, 92–95
Loncar, M. 58

Mahara 67
metacognition 68, 118
Meyer, E. 18
Microsoft Word 58, 60
mobile devices 58
Moodle 26, 58, 66
Moya, S. S. 29
multimodal digital portfolios 13
My Story Book Maker 62

natgeokids.com 130
National Association for the Education of Young Children 69
Navarre, A. 70
Nearpod 66, 121, 130
Nicolaidou, I. 18

O'Malley, J. M. 29
online assessment systems 15
online gaming 58
open-source tools 15, 66, 71

Padlet 26, 43, 67, 131
pedagogy, portfolio 37–38
personalised learning 67–68
Pigai 58
portable devices 58
portfolios 1–2; applications of 5; collection, selection, and reflection in 3; definitions related to 3–4, *4*; digital *versus* print 3–4, *4*; evolution of 5–8, *6*; *see also* digital portfolios; print portfolios
practicality of portfolio-based curriculum 31–33
primary trait scoring 46, **48**
print portfolios 1, 3–4, *4*; applications of 5; evolution of 5, *6*
privacy issues 136–137
process approach to writing instruction 24–25
process digital portfolios 18
process-oriented portfolio classrooms 32

product-based portfolio classrooms
  31–32
 pros and cons of digital portfolios
  16–17

Quizizz 118, 130–131
Quizlet 70

rationale for digital portfolios: origin,
  features, types, and medium in
  12–15, *13*, **15**; socio-constructivism
  10–11, *12*
Reading Rockets 98
Readwritethink 113
REFLECT Initiative 6
reflection 3, 14, 31–32, 135
reflective learning 68
reflective thinking 11, *12*
Renwick, M. 71
rubric construction for assessment
  45–50, **47–49**
Ryan, M. 44

SAMR model 70–71, *71*
Schoology 43, 45, 67
Seesaw 67, 69, 71–73, 98; for
  bottom-up processing skills
  development 89–92, *91–92*; parental
  involvement on 95–96; preparing
  students for use of 95; for top-down
  processing skills development
  92–95; use in pre-school learners'
  literacy development 88–96
selection 3
self-authoring software 15
self-reflection by students 40–41, 54, 70
self-regulated learning in writing of
  primary school learners: digital
  portfolio programme for 104–105;
  introduction to 100–111; preparing
  students for use of digital portfolios
  for 110–111; principles of using
  digital portfolios for 111–112;
  resources on 113–114; school setting
  for 102; school-based English-
  language writing curriculum and
  102–104; strategies for developing
  105–110
self-regulated learning promoted with
  e-feedback 58–62

showcase portfolios 14, **15**
site of integration 13
social learning 70
social media 6, 58, 138–139
socio-constructivism 10–11, *12*, 56
Sparklebox.com 113
standardised digital portfolio
  assessment (SDPA) 39, **40**
storytelling 60–62
Student Assessment Repository
  (STAR) 120
student engagement 137–138
Sun, Y. C. 18

technical aspects of digital portfolios
  58, 139
Telegram 139
*Territory-wide System Assessment
  (TSA) for English Language* 119
TikTok 139
tools, digital portfolio 143–145;
  collaborative learning
  68–69; criteria for selecting
  appropriate 69–71, *71*; learning
  management systems 58, 60, 66–67,
  88–89, 105, 110–111, 120–121;
  mini-research task on 78, **79–81**;
  open-source 15, 66; overview of
  66–67; personalised learning 67–68;
  rationale behind use of 67–69;
  reflective learning 68; software
  74–78; for three common types of
  digital portfolios 71–74
top-down processing skills
  development 87, 92–95
types of digital portfolios 14, **15**,
  71–74

vignettes: blending assessment
  and learning of writing in
  secondary school language
  classrooms 116–131; pre-school
  learners' literacy development
  86–99; self-regulated learning in
  writing of primary school learners
  100–114
Vygotsky, L. 10

web-based portfolios 15
websites 71, 73–74

WeChat 60
WhatsApp 58, 60, 139
Wiki 70, 138
Wix 43, 73
WordHippo 114
WordPress 71–72
Wordwall 99
work portfolios 14, **15**
writing evaluation using digital portfolios 38–41, **40**

writing instruction 24–25, 133–135; *See also* self-regulated learning in writing of primary school learners

Yancey, K. B. 13–15, 19
YouTube 99, 138

zone of proximal development (ZPD) 10–11, *12*
Zoom 44, 75

For Product Safety Concerns and Information please contact our EU representative GPSR@taylorandfrancis.com
Taylor & Francis Verlag GmbH, Kaufingerstraße 24, 80331 München, Germany

www.ingramcontent.com/pod-product-compliance
Lightning Source LLC
Chambersburg PA
CBHW070550170426
43201CB00012B/1784